Golden PROSE & Poetry

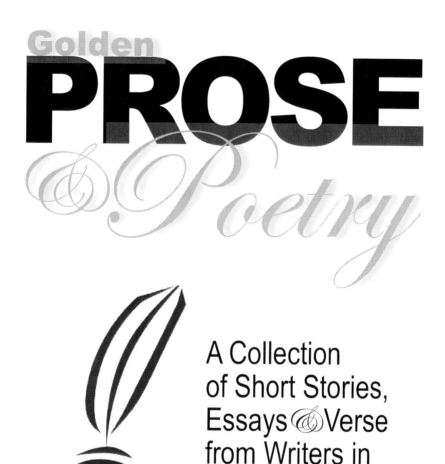

A Collection of Short Stories, Essays & Verse from Writers in Northern California

PRETTY ROAD PRESS
in association with
Northern California Publishers & Authors

Golden Prose & Poetry:
A Collection of Short Stories, Essays & Verse from Writers in Northern California

Published by
Pretty Road Press
P.O. Box 273
Folsom California 95763
www.PrettyRoadPress.com

This book is independently published by Pretty Road Press in arrangement with individual members of Northern California Publishers & Authors: www.NorCalPA.org

Printed in the United States of America

ISBN 978-0-9826014-5-7

17 16 15 14 13   5 4 3 2 1

to readers
in the Golden State of California,
with thanks from
members of
Northern California Publishers & Authors

Contents

Margo **King Lenson**

Margo King Lenson lives in Vacaville, California, with her husband, Malcolm, and three contented cats. She published her first short story, "The Me You See," as a freshman in college for a psychology anthology edited by her professor.

Decades later, she indie published the book series, *Pacific Voices Talk Series: Conversations of American Experience, Volumes 1-4*, through her business, Tui Communications.

Besides her books, Margo has spoken and given presentations at California campuses to raise consciousness of Pacific Peoples living off-island. What Islanders left behind in Oceania to find in the continental United States is usually the subject of her work, but in "Sexing the Professor," she explores the unfulfilled promise of a literary spell.

Margo can be reached through Northern California Publishers & Authors.

Sexing the Professor

On a warm Wednesday evening of spring, I had stayed late after work to type a short paper for my final Modern Poetry class: a simple response piece, three pages, combining Gertrude Stein's words and Cezanne's *Mont Sainte-Victoire* in an artistic match. Fabricating a Parisian encounter in 1903, I squared-off these pugnacious outsider-artists and had a blast. My pleasure in writing was finally back.

For years I had put my poli sci degree to work for serious pay only to find out that being paid to write stinks. Still, being paid well for my "communication skills" had its pluses, not the least of which was my own office and an assistant posted outside to protect me from sales people.

I was working then at the California District Association in downtown San Rafael where I could walk to the San Rafael Mission during lunch and sit on the hard wooden pews in the chapel's adobe-cushioned silence. I had much to pray for (humility, patience, compassion), but more often I had closed my eyes and thought about Neil Gleich who taught modern poetry. Over the semester, the young professor's devoted occupation at the woodsy, wisteria-vined and wild-gardened Dominican College had convinced me that I was living a lie — well, two lies: one, my faked satisfaction with my boss Elaine's effusive praise of my work; and two, my smiling contentment being home with Martin night after night, snuggled against him, watching *Kojak*. Not that I didn't need to work and didn't need my husband, but neither inspired me to write: no stories, no poetry, no spontaneous scribbling, no interesting observations. I had to do something to get back on an honest writing track, otherwise I would simply disappear. Poof, into thin air, gone, as if I never existed.

In the hidden, old-moneyed part of San Rafael, I had first found the four-storied slat-board Dominican Convent, then, behind it, scattered campus buildings on hilly, forested grounds. Despite the $200 fee per unit, I registered for the three-unit undergraduate night class that called me to its pentameter ranks, Modern Poetry. It was certainly cheaper than a shrink over a four-month period. And one night a week detached from Martin's side spared me from numbering the times Kojak yelled, "Crocker!"

Six short-papers plus other writings later, I had no regrets. On this final day, in fact, I was expecting more than the abrupt end of class thanks to William Carlos Williams. This most paternal poet of the genre and Neil's hypnotic lecture on Williams's "overheard speech or overlooked landscape" inspired me to write a seductive critique filled with double-entendre, innuendo, and invitation intended for Neil's tender response. Usually, his marginal notes came back to me in lengthy engagement, prefaced by fixing the hour in his delicate scrawl: "It's 2:17 a.m. as I read this . . . ," "1:42 in the morning and your comments infuriate . . . ," "Just past midnight, but I will try to understand you. . . ."

When he had returned the Williams paper to me late in the previous class, running out the door to meet with the dean, I read his piqued message, "WCW committed to his art true love of life . . . how can you dismiss the simple beauty of 'The Young Housewife' concerns me. Must discuss with you next week!"

On this Wednesday, thrilled with the anticipation of seeing Professor Gleich one-on-one, I handed in my final Stein-Cezanne paper and sat at the far end of the seminar table opposite Neil. The ten other students had drawn a line between me and them all semester long. I was the mature, working, married one; they the young, extremely bright, and bored children of the Catholic elite. Once again, they clustered on either side of the table, so that I always seemed to be just visiting, a fringe-faction of one. I was used to their cliquish high-school treatment, having attended an all-girls Catholic high before they were born. Such exclusionary habits die hard, although given my odd singularity, I couldn't blame the girls. The idea that I was merely taking a class for pleasure was barely tolerable to them.

But we, the students, were tacitly united on one towering point: the course was an incredibly tough one. Along with tackling the difficult material, Neil made the class even more so with his strict demands (a paper per poet, a compilation of creative notes, a presentation, a final paper of our choosing). Whenever possible, I was reading poetry, writing, thinking, and fantasizing about Neil, his tan face above me like a cloud. God, I loved him for his severity, for his passion, for his striking German face, the brightly tired blue-eyes, the familiar circles beneath them from too many cigarettes, too many late nights, too many insomniac explications.

Often, during class he would direct his piercing lectures exclusively at me, no doubt fed by my rapt attention and hungry interest. Glancing about the table, I saw that more than half of the students were woefully indifferent to the rhythms of truth and beauty, sleeping with their eyes opened. What they missed of the handsome professor's sensitive and dramatic offerings, I lapped up greedily, nourished and alive from an uneventful workday and routine marriage.

At the end of this Wednesday night, I gathered my books and notes slowly while the rest of the students hurriedly cleared out *sans* any fond goodbyes. I walked up to Neil. We had never spoken alone together. Up to this point all of our communication had been textual and safely structured.

"Wanted to see me, Professor? About Williams, I mean."

He acted startled by my darkly fish-eyed presence confronting him and gave a quick, distracted nod before pushing up his rolled cuff to check his watch. Reaching into his khaki pants, he pulled out a crumpled pack of Camels. Finding it empty, he threw it away, missing the garbage can by a mile. He had lectured past ten and seemed tired but relieved that he was done with the lot of us, except for me.

As if recognizing whom I was for the first time, he smiled and bowed graciously. His outstretched hand let me out of the classroom, down the long steps, and outside into the night. A full bewitching moon beckoned. The scent of gardenias, roses, and grass wet with dew struck our senses like a shot. The professor directed me towards a bench glowing by the exterior lights of the library. A ceramic sculptured Madonna and Child glistened in the moonlight above us, taunting us to pray and be good.

I thought of Martin, his soft kiss of this morning, the you-and-me-babe kiss of married life. Four years of contentment and happiness so pure instantly dissipated in the steamy anticipation of being with Neil Gleich, professor and poet. How many times had I delved into dangerous imaginings of our contrasting bodies and hairs tangled together in the white, mussed sheets of Motel Sleaze? I couldn't count them. I couldn't think as he took the cigarette I offered, lit mine and brushed my fingers, the blond hairs on his hands glistening.

Yes, I loved Martin — and disdained him. Ultimately, he was always there, unconditionally the same, whereas Neil made me write and work and think of poetry as more than pretty words on the page, but the stuff of mind and life beyond quotidian ritual.

"So, Professor, do you think I am misreading Williams? Just because I think he's a wimp?" I knew what I was doing, provoking Neil to argue with me.

"Why do you talk like this? Why do you write such hostile papers? This is what I want to speak to you about, Ms. Londin. You think Gertrude Stein sadistic, Robert Creeley insufferable, and Dr. Williams a wimp. I don't understand you. I know you're capable of sensitive close-readings, but you can't mean half the things you write."

Irritated, he began to turn towards the orchard of olive trees ringing the campus housing where he lived. It never occurred to me that he would just walk away without expressing any connection, let alone affection for me, considering that he practically engulfed my body-language in class.

"Are you leaving?" I asked, incredulously. "Is this all you have to say to me? That I'm insincere and hostile?"

"What else? What do you think? You've earned an A in the class; don't worry."

A yard of force hung between us. Its gravity pulled from the ground, invisibly dragging me to imagine myself on my knees before him, my arms braced at his waist. But the professor repelled seduction.

"What about Olson?" I blurted. "I thought he was brilliant. He's absolutely perfect for tonight." My face shone hotly as I lit another cigarette, and recited:

> "O souls, burn
> alive, burn now
> that you may forever
> have peace, have what you crave"

I waited in silence and added, "Good ole Olson." I stood, seizing the handle of my briefcase like a barbell. It would be I who would leave first, not Neil.

The lights of the library were extinguished, slipping us into steep darkness beneath redwood branches. Far glass-doors opened, tumbling forth stray students and tired workers into the night. I stepped back as Sister Rita, dean of students, flashed her grey eyes inquisitively at Neil, a junior faculty member, in my company, a suited woman, smoking and unflinching. She acknowledged us both by name, said goodnight and hurried in the direction of the convent. Her traditional nun's habit roped by a huge rosary remained a clinging image in my mind as I faced Neil.

For sixteen weeks I'd listened to his wise lectures and learned beyond my expectations. His sometimes profane visual aids — the slide show of nudes, the art books and pictures of phallic modern architecture — all ostensibly meant to amplify the liberation of self in modern art, exposed his true erotic side to me. His intricate instruction on Freudian, scientific, and political thrusts of early twentieth century cited their synthesis in poetry and a new treatment of words as illusive, slippery, lying objects. One could only trust experience for truth and reality, specifically, experience of a sexual nature. I perceived Neil's lustful conviction on this matter as no less intense than my own.

"I want you, Neil." I said. "Just for an hour?" I longed for him in darkness thick with religion, wealth, and academia. Vernal traces of liaisons in ivy-covered dorms, trysts on the moistened grass behind the hedges protested the holy atmosphere.

"An hour, Miriam? Are you sick? Does marriage, fidelity, family mean nothing to you? My wife is waiting for me. I have an eight-month-old daughter."

The wind had picked up a little heat and rustled through tall dry eucalyptus with long, leafy sounds. I snuffed out my cigarette, shifted my briefcase, and repositioned my clutch purse securely under my arm.

> "I speak downfall, the ball of my foot
> on the neck of the earth, the hardsong
> of the rise of all trees, the jay
> who uses the air . . ."

"Olson, again," I said.

Neil stared at me. "Do you still want to talk about Williams? "The Young Housewife?"

As if we were in a contest, he recited its key lines:

"The noiseless wheels of my car
rush with a crackling sound over
dried leaves as I bow and pass smiling . . ."

"Boring," I said, and walked towards the student parking lot, over-sexed and wanting.

Jeff**Parsons**

J eff Parsons uses humor to help him avoid life's complications. Winning several humorous speech contests inspired him to write a true-life story about his most unusual hotel stay. Warning: provocative underwear is involved.

Alternatively, Jeff writes horror stories to confront his fears. He has appeared in the *Bonded by Blood IV and V* anthologies. SNM Horror Magazine released Jeff's debut book of incredibly scary stories, titled *Algorithm of Nightmares*, in December 2012.

When nothing works to make the monsters go away, Jeff bravely flees in terror, living to fight yet another day, whilst eating lots of chocolate to console himself.

Despite all evidence to the contrary, Jeff lives a reasonably quiet life within the fine city of Rocklin. Jeff_95630@yahoo.com is his email address.

Ain't Nothing Gonna Break My Stride

Flashback to 1986. Click. What was that sound? A closing door? I'm standing in front of a locked door. I vaguely recognize this door. It won't open.

"No, no, no. I just want to go back to sleep!"

Okay, now I'm fully awake, outside my hotel room, in the hallway, sometime late at night. I've been sleepwalking. Yes, sleepwalking?

"Wait. Oh my God!"

I'm dressed only in my red Speedo underwear. That's it. Let's just say, like a good English composition, it is long enough to cover the subject, but brief enough to make it interesting.

"Oh, noooooo! Open the door. Open the door. Open the door!" It won't open.

My throat knots up. "What. Am. I. Going. To. Do?"

I carefully review my survival checklist. Hmm. I realize I'm going die of embarrassment! Terrible way to go. Very messy. As a shy 25 year old man, I'm not okay with this.

"What can I do?" I ask myself.

I could wait here until some people happen along. That would be an unusual encounter, no doubt. They would probably run away screaming. Worse yet, they'd point and laugh. Death by humiliation seems to have come in two varieties tonight: 1) immediate humiliation under the brand of an unwitting sexual pervert, or 2) prolonged humiliation, leaving a permanent mental scar to my manly ego. All options looked grim.

"Wait!" I tell myself. "I could knock on someone's door."

"Help me! It's 2 a.m.! I'm hot, sweaty, and I'm in my underwear! And I want — sniffle — a hug."

Hmm! When the security SWAT team arrives, I'm thinking they'll say something like, "Boy, we're gonna enjoy hurting you real bad."

That would be death by— Oh my God! I can't even imagine it, let alone say it.

Factoid: milling about aimlessly will never help a near-naked man.

I knew what I had to do: retrieve an electronic keycard for my room. They dispense keycards at the front desk in the lobby. But— I was afraid. Yes, dreadfully afraid.

The door remained securely locked at the King of Prussia Hilton Hotel in über-conservative Pennsylvania. Imagine luxurious accommodations, fine dining, and high society people. In the lobby, a piano player entertains a soiree of sophisticated ladies and gents discussing the finer things in life over priceless champagne sipped from fluted glasses.

A popular disco nightclub also connects to the lobby, blaring reverberated vocals. At this tormented point of brain stirring, I imagine the entire Associated Press photography team, never without their cameras, waiting to crash the nightclub downstairs.

What would they think of the skinny pale-white man scurrying about in his undies? Well, it wasn't going to be pretty.

I sunk my shoulders, absolutely terrified, yet I found great resolve and courage, I forced myself to walk, albeit robotically. I trekked down the hallway headed for the lobby.

Some mental cog of mine slipped and stripped the rational gearbox in my brain. I experienced an outside-of-my-mind revelation. I just had to do this — go get a keycard — regardless of how I felt.

I started to pretend this whole episode was a dream — okay, truly a nightmare. I decided to play the part of a hero. Heroism means going on, despite overwhelming odds, not quite fearlessly — actually leaning redline towards crazy overload — but in a fully functional and effective manner.

Soon enough, my walk became a stroll. Standing tall, appearing outwardly to not have a care in the world, I owned the place. I was the King of Prussia, more empowered than a certain emperor who also once found himself naked.

Okay, I harbored some concerns and issues, but I was working my way through them.

Suddenly security cameras started rotating to follow me. "Whirr!" They move some more. "Scree—" They focus their lenses.

I made a royal entrance to my floor's foyer and summoned elevators with the down button. The foyer featured elegant French Renaissance style furniture. A chair and table led my eyes to a huge gold-rimmed mirror. How did I not notice the mirror when I first arrived in the foyer? I must have been fixated on pushing the down button.

I saw no king. I focused on a scared-spitless guy in his undies staring back at me. "What a freak! How surreal." I looked face-to face at my own fears. "May I choose death please, instead of this torture?"

No, apparently not. "Where was that elevator?"

Why does the elevator always take so long to arrive when you're anxious and impatient? I whistled to pass the time. Now I know what eternity feels like.

Whistling sounds horrible when you're nervous. And then, when you realize that you're nervous, that makes the whistling even worse — absolutely dreadful.

"Ding!"

An elevator door suddenly opened. I admit it: I squeaked out a strangled scream. "Ahh! Oh! No people!"

Was I lucky or what? I leapt into the car and stabbed the button to close the door — repeatedly. With manic passion, I stabbed it.

The doors finally closed. Nothing happened. Eventually, I realized that I also had to push the destination button: L is for lobby

My mission was to get to the lobby unnoticed. Down, down, down, the indicator lights flickered to my doom. "Go to L." It sounded like the British cursing to me. "What the L am I doing in this predicament?"

It's all definitely an L word, the soon-to-be low point in my life.

Thinking one step ahead, I decided that if I encountered someone, I'd calmly say something inappropriately normal: "Hey, how do I get to the spa?" And then, while they're distracted by my non-sequitur query, I'd quickly slink away like a ninja, a mostly-naked ninja, but, still a ninja. The plan sounded intelligent enough.

"Ding!"

My heartbeat fluttered and stopped. I felt and heard, "Thump. Thump," then silence. My heart shifted into reverse. My body took a jumpstart back into panic mode.

The door opened. Could I be more naked facing the wide expanse of the lobby? Barely, I was exposed physically and naked mentally. Who knows? Maybe I could try spiritually as well, just go for the trifecta longshot of terror. If I include metaphorically, emphatically, and grammatically, I would be doomed before I even stepped out of the elevator.

I took possession of positive thoughts and kept on moving. "Don't stop or you're a dead man," I thought, but my optimism failed.

The lobby's size verged on the ridiculous. It qualified as a football field. I guess I had that going for me. Not.

I crossed a vast savannah of carpeting, abounding with a maze of furniture obstacles, brilliantly lit by the overhead chandeliers powered by sparkling megawatts.

The room provided no cover for other's imagination or my modesty. "Surprise! Here comes the naked man!" Even the walls were mocking me.

Okay, I was mostly-naked, but —sigh — what's the point, close enough really.

Background notes of Mozart's culturally refined music perfected the scene. The lobby was resplendent with an elegant social atmosphere, all for absolutely no one.

I was in a Twilight Zone episode where I was the only person left alive in the world. I found some comfort in the rationalization that maybe the lobby attendants were hiding. Or maybe they just couldn't see me yet.

Speaking of see-no-evil-nekked-ness, damn! I had been so traumatized by the ongoing situation that I only now realized that I had also left my glasses behind in the room. I am myopic. Let's just say that the world is blurry at a distance. Close up, not so bad. "If I can't see them," I rationalized, "they can't see me, right?"

I remembered to breathe because I was getting forgetful in these climactic seconds. With fresh air, I pressed onward to the front desk.

It seemed a second eternity to get there. You know those dreams where you are in the third grade, and, for some reason, you haven't been listening during an arithmetic lesson? Suddenly, your teacher calls upon you to solve a problem on the blackboard. That obliges the slow walk to the front of the class. "No, no, no! Please, not that."

Time and space became slow, drippy, and gooey, like molasses-flavored taffy that your sister offers to you after it's been ABC'd (Already Been Chewed). Fuzzy with pocket lint also comes to mind.

Eventually, I rang the bell on the counter of the front desk. It sounded much too loud, too attention getting. I became nervous that it might attract the indigenous lobby people. They are drawn to these sounds. They would emerge as a pack from the shadows.

I quickly scoped out the surrounding area. As far as I could tell, I was alone. Hooray for poor vision! Probably I was on several candid cameras at this point.

In typical fashion, a distinguished, tuxedoed man magically appeared from the desk's backroom while I was squinting about with my back turned.

"Sir?" he drawled, scaring me considerably and rigorously testing my potty training. I passed. No problems.

I slowly turned and said in my best what-the-heck-just-happened-to-me mode, "Oh, why h-e-l-l-o, I seem to have misplaced my keycard. May I have another one?"

"Why, of course, sir."

He vanished into the backroom and came back out immediately. He presented an electronic keycard to me.

"Wow! Damn good service here!" I thought.

"Thank you," I whispered, in awe of his power. I thought this approach would sound more dignified than, say, "Dear (random hotel employee), thank you, thank you, thank you for saving me from a fate worse than death. I owe you my life. Hey, let's party together sometime. Call me maybe."

He nodded and returned to the backroom, smiling in an odd way that put my mind to thinking.

"Wait a minute! How could he have created my electronic keycard so fast? I didn't even tell him my room number! Oh My God, he knew! He was watching me on the security cameras that were following my every movement. Arr, and this is all being recorded somewhere! (Note to self: never get curious about what may have shown up on YouTube.)"

With as much dignity as I could muster, I marched back to my room, avoiding any close encounters of the naked kind and thinking, "Wow, did I really just go to the lobby in my undies?"

Keycard in hand, I opened my room's locked door to three valuable lessons:

1) Always wear pajamas when sleeping in a hotel.

2) When you find yourself in public in nothing but your underwear, try to behave with dignity, poise, and grace.

3) Despite the common nightmare we all share of being nearly naked in public, it's actually not that bad.

Kimberly A. **Edwards**

Kimberly A. Edwards writes on cross-cultural issues, lifestyle and seniors, event planning, meetings, and boardsmanship. Her print credits include: *Cosmopolitan, Seventeen, Senior Spectrum,* the *Times of India,* the *Sacramento Bee, International Travel News, Sacramento News and Review, Training and Development Journal,* and the IBPA (Independent Book Publishers Association) *Independent.*

Recently, her "Tapping into Twitter Expertise" was selected for IBPA's ebook, *The Book Publishers Toolkit: 10 Practical Pointers for Independent and Self Publishers.*

Kimberly serves as an officer for the California Writers Club, Sacramento Branch. Recently she retired from the California Department of Education, where she coordinated programs including the California Teachers of the Year and crafted the "Noon Hour with a Local Author" series.

Contact her at KimberlyEdwards00@comcast.net.

Redeemed in the Sacred Valley of the Incas

The day had been like no other: four hours on the early train from Cuzco to Aguas Calientes, then a ride on a bus that spiraled up rugged terrain, and finally the hike through mist to Machu Picchu. Now, on the return trip to Cuzco, the train stopped in the village of Ollantaytambo, where the scent of jasmine lured me to the open window as the sun sank into the eucalyptus trees.

On the station platform, an indigenous woman carried handicrafts bundled in a shawl. Something about her smile made me feel as if I knew her.

"Mañana," I uttered, assuring her that a tour scheduled for the next day would bring me back when I would be more alert and prepared to buy.

She nodded, conveying that our connection bridged language and culture. As I started to shuffle back to my seat, she held up a doll dressed in white and embracing a baby alpaca.

"Cuánto?" I asked, against my better judgment.

"Doce soles."

I sighed, my knees wobbling as fatigue set in.

"Diez," she teased, lowering the price. Her eyes, framed by glossy black hair, emitted a friendliness that made me want to oblige. She passed the doll through the window.

I handed this precious acquisition to Conchita, a fellow passenger, as I fished in my side pocket, but found no Peruvian *soles*. A faint whistle sounded. I felt for my pouch under my shirt. The locomotive hissed. I unzipped both purse pockets. All I found was a five-dollar U.S. bill.

"I have change," called the woman outside, brandishing a Peruvian bill.

A whistle shrieked, signaling imminent departure. Passengers gathered around me.

"Give her the American bill," coaxed a short man.

"What's five dollars to you, an American?" pressed a tall man. "She's only asking for three."

The words from these advisers mixed with the rising roar of the locomotive, creating fog in my brain.

"Hurry," yelled both men, flanked by gathering onlookers. "Give her the money!"

I tore into my money belt. The crowd dispensed more opinions, but my mounting panic prevented logical thought. "I— I can't find my Peruvian money," I blurted.

"Hummmph!" chided the spectators in English and Spanish.

Outside, a look of confusion fell over the face of the woman. Eucalyptus leaves began to move as the train crawled from the station.

"Then we'll have to return this baby," declared Conchita, dangling the doll out the window as the engine growled.

I turned away, mortified. Gasps arose from the spectators as Conchita pulled back her elbow. Trees began to pass. She flung her arm forward, launching my intended purchase into the Andean sky. "There she goes, poor, poor dolly!" she lamented, followed by an imagined thud on the tracks, which the group mimicked in moans.

I slinked to my seat. My hat couldn't cover my face enough. I wanted to disappear. Here I, an American tourist, had dishonored a local merchant, but more importantly, a person who had trusted me. In a fury I ripped through my money bag to discover my Peruvian bills exactly where they belonged.

As the train descended into the twilight of the Sacred Valley of the Incas, embers flickered in the distance. My mind replayed the scene of the stranger who believed in a passing train before seeing her craftsmanship purged like garbage. If only I had handed over the five-dollar U.S. bill. Why had I failed to comprehend a simple concept? At a moment of need, wavering between peaks and plains, I had lost my wits at the window. When decisiveness counted, I had withered like a hibiscus after a drizzle.

I summoned up all the times I had let someone down, but none so disgracefully as this. Again and again I beat myself up. For the rest of my life, I would recall the disbelief in the woman's dark eyes upon hearing that I couldn't find money. If only I could have that minute back. As the flames outside lowered and my mind kneaded every emotion, I realized the only way to quell my regret.

The following afternoon, returning to Ollantaytambo, I focused on a new personal plan. I followed the others plodding along the Incan cobblestones that led to the heart of the village. Jasmine curled up the adobe brick buildings, diffusing a familiar scent. Ahead on the hill loomed the ancient Incan stronghold the group planned to explore.

While they ascended, I stayed below, where an open market offered hand-made wares. I moved methodically from booth to booth, relishing each woman's work, hearing how each person knitted *chuno* caps, alpaca scarves, and gloves. All the while I tried to muster the nerve to inquire about the woman who stood on the station platform the previous day.

At one of the last stands, dolls lay arranged in a row. Two were boy figures, of which I had seen few. They wore intricate beaded caps.

I paused to inspect this unusual work. Then I spotted the woman who had dwelled in my mind all night. She did not recognize me, but her demeanor was as warm as I remembered.

"Was your doll thrown from the train yesterday?" I asked.

She blinked several times.

"That was me," I admitted.

Startled, she stared back as her mind pieced my face into an open train window in the setting sun. Her smile spread from ear to ear. She pointed to a doll on a nearby stand. "There she is. I repaired her last night by replacing the smashed baby alpaca with a bull that will bring luck and protection."

"I'll buy her," I said.

She passed me the doll and pinned a little drum to the white dress. "For you," she whispered.

Watching from a table, three young boys sat very straight. I asked if these were her sons, and she said yes. She signaled to a girl of about twelve — her daughter. The girl, with shiny hair like her mother's, brought over a basket with more dolls.

An hour later, I stood at the base of the mountain watching the group descend. On my shoulder I carried a new bag containing six dolls, all from my friend. Sunlight spilled over the ruins, reminding me that the past brings meaning to the present through nature and humanity.

Often in life we miss opportunities to redeem ourselves. In Ollantaytambo I was granted a second chance. Of all my dolls, none is as treasured as the one I wounded on the rails. The woman whose name I will never know granted me more than a travel memento. Seven years later, I cherish the privilege of righting a wrong at the foot of the Incan fortress.

Frances **Kakugawa**

Frances H. Kakugawa, award winning author and poet who currently resides in Sacramento, was born and raised on the Big Island of Hawaii in Kapoho, which was demolished by lava when she was eighteen. She taught in Michigan, Hawaii, and  Micronesia and served as a teacher, trainer, curriculum writer, and lecturer for the University of Hawaii.

In 2002, she was recognized in *Living Legacy: Outstanding Women of the 20th Century in Hawaii.* Her children's books and her *Kapoho: Memoir of a Modern Pompeii* have received awards from the Hawaii Publishers Award for Excellence and from Northern California Publishers & Authors. Today, she continues to write, conducts poetry writing support groups for caregivers, gives writing workshops for adults and children, and lectures on caregiving and poetry throughout the United States.

Visit her website at www.FrancesK.org or read her blog at FrancesKakugawa.WordPress.com. Also connect at Facebook.com//FrancesKakugawa.

Junkyard for Writers

A bricholeur collects things often called junk by others. His backyard looks like the city dump with old empty paint cans, old shelving, buckets of old nails, discarded tires, broken computers, and old pots and pans. There is no order to how they are placed in the yard. A junkyard offers no rhyme or reason.

A bricholeur doesn't see junk; he looks at his yard and sees possibilities. He takes a little of this and a little of that and creates. Sometimes it doesn't work, and a new design or vision is necessary. Other times, it fits just as imagined. Sometimes, the best of times, a bricholeur is totally surprised by his own creation. I once watched a bricholeur build two compost bins with collected discarded materials from the neighborhood trash.

Imagine if you were to write with a junkyard mentality. Take the bricholeur's advice. Look at your own junkyard of collected experiences, feelings, ideas, thoughts, imagination, knowledge, passion, and love of writing. Keep feeding that junkyard by living life with open arms and an open mind, experimenting, remembering, preserving, observing, thinking.

Then take the only tool in hand, language, and become a bricholeur in your junkyard. Just as a bricholeur uses all the right tools for his bricholeuring, so must you. Use the most beautiful and creative language possible with artistry and imagination.

All the words needed to create a story or poem are found in a dictionary at your fingertips. They are listed and defined. It's how you string these words together that creates this magic called writing. All the words found in Nobel- and Pulitzer-prize winning books are available to us.

This means we must also have knowledge of how language works. This is why the writer's craft becomes important, encompassing all the literary devices and elements used by writers: metaphors, symbolism, various types of plots, acute images, settings, climaxes, and the like.

So we read and write and write and read to explore how best to use language. Just as one can't learn to swim by standing by the poolside, wishing he could swim, with a *How to Swim* manual in his hand, a writer must take that pen and write.

Become a bricholeur and have fun with your writing, just as I had fun writing this poem:

What is a Poem?

Write, write, write, I say.
But what is a poem, you ask.
And how do I write?
What can a poem hold?

It is a fragile shopping bag
    rice paper thin, egg shell thin
        but oh, don't let its appearance
           stop you from shopping.

Too heavy a load
    may rip right through
        and splat! It's all at your feet, or
           rolling into a ditch, or
               too shattered into pieces
                   for all the King's men and all the King's horses.

There is really no way of knowing
　　what weight it will hold
　　　　or the number of items
　　　　　　or size.

So place it gently, slowly,
　　　　into the bag.
　　　　　　Test it for while, hold it close to your heart,
　　　　　　　swing it away to and fro,
　　　　　　　carry it a mile, feel it roll around the bag,
　　　　　　　　let its weight bounce against your knees.
　　　　　　　　skip, run, walk,
　　　　　　　and if the bag is still intact
　　　　　　　　you know the content's just about right.

And what do you do with bags torn apart
　　and content scattered at your feet,
　　　　with no one near to give you a hand?
　　　　　　Why, just get a wheelbarrow, any color will do,
　　　　　　haul it away

　　　　　　And go shopping again.

Joyce **Mason**

Joyce Mason is a writer and astrologer. She has published three e-books on astrology and contributed articles to numerous astrological publications, including *The Mountain Astrologer*.

 Joyce's blog, *The Radical Virgo* (www.radicalvirgo.com) features more than half of the four hundred articles she has written for her own and others' blogs online. In 2005, Joyce won first place for her memoir proposal at the Yosemite Writers' Conference. Her mystery short "Digital" appeared in the 2008 *Capitol Crimes,* an anthology featuring works of the local members of Sisters in Crime.

Two other books are in line for publication: a new astrology book and her first mystery novel, *The Crystal Ball.* Visit her website at www.JoyceMason.com.

Joyce lives with her husband Tim and fur family in Rocklin, California.

Cruel Embroidery

How we experience life has a lot to do with how we see ourselves. The psyche is a canvas, a musical score, or an embroidery sampler. Fill in your favorite metaphor. Nothing can come into our lives that we do not paint, write, or stitch first with the invisible medium of mind. When self-image goes off track—especially if it goes way off—life derails with it.

Thus was the strange case of Miss Ewa Cardy, dubbed the neighborhood witch by children in her tiny town of Azalee, Massachusetts. Azalee is a short ride from Salem, where other women accused of being witches once were hung more than three centuries ago for what largely turned out to be terrible rumors.

Fitting the stereotype, Miss Cardy's house looked haunted, strewn with enough cobwebs to house a nation of spiders. It crawled with cats, too, most of them black. Miss Ewa was reclusive, and children were scared of her. Their mantra when speaking of her was the current common expression for *icky*, a spin on her name — *ewwww*. They knew full well she pronounced her name *Evva*, but they said *Ewwwwa* just for spite.

Little did they know that no one could be more disgusted with Ewa Cardy than Ewa Cardy herself. Anyone versed in human psychology, even the pop variety, would know it from these few facts: Miss Cardy was an extreme introvert, clinically depressed. She did not like herself or anyone else. These sad realities added to her infamy. Most people were happy to avoid her like a door-to-door evangelist, except for the occasional times when her blight of a house stirred her neighbors to contact the authorities in an effort to make her "do something."

Even with the force of the law, the arm of the small City of Azalee could do little. Most people preferred not find out what Ewa Cardy was doing in there, behind closed doors, even those authorities who had a right to pound on them. After all, she was a million years old, and it did not look good to be mean to old ladies, even old ladies who were mean themselves. Mayor Anthony Bisco was hell bent on another term of office. Coming down hard on old ladies, even a lady who was a notorious and nasty old bat, would be poor politics.

Miss Cardy snapped at children. Her herd of cats changed so often that rumor had it, she killed off the extras when the population got too dense. In the end, Ewa Cardy was a tough old bird, maybe even a vulture, but she was something—*someone*—you just had to live with.

Luckily for her neighbors, Ewa Cardy used her garbage service on occasion. Sightings of her were rarer than Boston-area fans of the New York Yankees. To escape their eyes, she must have pulled her toter to the curb on shaky old-lady limbs after dark, on nights before the truck was due. One spring Wednesday, garbage man Jesse Fordyce found a large object wrapped in trash bags inside Miss Cardy's black toter. He and his wingman, Wayne Averitt, had to look, holding their noses, nearly certain of what they would find underneath the matching black plastic. It was a body all right. It was small, questionably adult. Did Ewa Cardy actually kill small animals and children?

It was what happened before the discovery that made the Ewa Cardy Garbage Incident more complicated —a life before her legend and trashcan drew swarms of gendarmes and reporters from as far away as Boston, all to the doorstep of her haunted house in their gooseflesh.

A coincidence of light and dark had merged late the previous summer. A family had moved in less than a block away from Ewa Cardy—a family that could only be described as Ozzie and Harriet on Tulip Street. They had one daughter, a blonde who looked like Patty McCormack in *The Bad Seed* before you knew there was anything bad about her—and in the case of Mary Ann Mefford, there wasn't anything.

She was Little Mary Sunshine, a child so pure her teeth sparkled when she smiled. Stars sparkled in her bright blue eyes, complementing the light show. Thirteen years old, Mary Ann was known for long walks in the neighborhood, trying to find someone to talk to till school started and she could make new friends. She would often offer to walk neighbors' dogs or push a baby cart to give moms a break.

Maybe it was the magnetism we all have to our opposite, but Mary Ann was transfixed by Ewa Cardy's house. She had never mentioned her fascination to anyone else, and she had not been warned by the neighbors or their frightened children about what was behind the spooky, run-down eyesore.

One Saturday Little Mary Sunshine could stand it no longer. She collected a few dollars of her meager allowance and visited the farmer's market. She bought a few vegetables and fruits. Mary Ann placed them in a plain, but functional old basket she found in her family's garage. Unaware of the irony that it is the newcomer who usually receives the basket of goodies from the established neighbors, she hummed a song and walked toward the haunt. With love and curiosity in her heart, Mary Ann walked right up to the home of Ewa Cardy. She knocked on the door in a way that was eager, but not pushy. After three knocks with long waits in-between, the door creaked.

***

"Who are you and what do you want?"

The voice from behind the door was cross and sounded more annoyed than curious.

Mary Ann remained as steadfast in her sweetness as Ewa Cardy stood fixed in her crabbiness. It would take months before the girl got her toe inside the haunted house. She was lucky Miss Cardy let her leave the basket on the doorstep before she sent her on her way. Mary Ann Mefford sensed an opening, one that had to precede all others.

By Thanksgiving, Mary Ann had acquired new friends at school, but she devoted at least an hour, twice a week, to visiting Miss Cardy. If she had anyone to tell, the recluse would now have admitted she looked forward to the girl's visits and the spoils of the errands the child offered to do for her.

"Here's your cough medicine," Mary Ann said to the woman one day, emptying a bag from the local pharmacy. When Miss Cardy offered her a five-dollar bill, she refused to take it.

"Consider it an early Christmas present."

Ewa Cardy had not celebrated Christmas since she was a teenager.

One millimeter at a time, Miss Sunshine got next to the old woman. She kept it to herself. By now she had heard all the awful rumors about Ewa. Even though she knew them to be untrue, she also knew she was fighting a fierce force field of negative sentiment. It was too big for her to handle alone, so she just went about having her own experiences with the woman. Not even her parents knew where she went when she was off to "see a friend," nor were they curious as to details in this neighborhood where people rarely locked their cars or houses.

Long about January "Miss Ewa" — as she lightened up enough to let the girl call her — began showing Mary Ann her embroidery. The colors were subdued, the stitchery lush, but taken together the scenes depicted were disturbing. The stitches often portrayed a girl alone in the darkest of colors. Skies were cloudy. The works were so heavy. Mary Ann feared they would fall off the wall in their frames by the sheer weight of the depression they emanated.

In one picture, a girl was leaving home—her parents had literally turned their backs on her. Another showed a young mother alone, fighting against a snow flurry, her infant child bundled and pressed to her bosom. Even the white of the snow did not lighten up the feeling of loss and oppression.

After several weeks of show and not much tell, Mary Ann finally got the nerve to ask Miss Ewa if the crewel embroidery was autobiographical.

"The young woman in all the stitchery? Is that you?"

Miss Ewa fidgeted in shock at being caught. For the longest time, she uttered not a word.

Now that she had become comfortable with Miss Ewa, Mary Ann could sit with her in silence. She let Miss Ewa come around at her own speed. They were alike in an odd way, both persistent and unconventional. Mary Ann was becoming Miss Ewa's friend, and in Azalee, Massachusetts, that was about as unconventional as a person could get.

On the day she asked the question about the embroidery, it took Miss Ewa nearly twenty minutes to say yes. After that, they were quiet, and Mary Ann left.

On her return a few days later, Miss Ewa seemed different — lighter and talkative to a degree that was entirely out of character. It was as though a dam had burst, and her story had to come out. Someone she could finally trust actually wanted to hear it.

Mary Ann listened through the winter months. Over their course, she learned Ewa Cardy's story by heart.

***

It was summer again, nearly a year since Mary Ann Mefford and her family moved to Azalee. A whole season had passed since the spring discovery of the body wrapped in Ewa Cardy's toter. In terms of local justice, the arm of the law was slow to arrest, but swift to set a trial for Miss Ewa, officially accused of murdering the man whose corpse was found in her trashcan.

"It's hard to date the remains without being sure of the conditions, where and how he was buried, or kept over the course of time," said the Coroner. "Our best estimate is that this is an adult male, though tiny in stature. We know he was disabled by birth defects. He appears to have died in his mid-twenties at least 40 years ago."

The courtroom took a collective gasp.

Her court-appointed attorney felt it was not wise to put Ewa Cardy on the stand because of the fierce local sentiment against her, a deep well of fear and hatred. He produced an unexpected character witness.

The court clerk recited the familiar legal litany: "Mary Ann Mefford, do you swear or affirm to tell the whole truth and nothing but the truth, so help you God?"

For Mary Ann Mefford, the oath was hardly necessary.

She unraveled the secrets behind Ewa Cardy's embroidery. A blind observer would have never guessed that the star witness for the defense was then only 14 years old.

"In her late teens, Miss Ewa got pregnant," said Mary Ann. "She was raped by a family member, a distant cousin. Her parents threw her out. She had to fend for herself. She was all alone."

Jurors and the full-house gallery were riveted. The judge accidentally dropped his pen and everyone jumped.

"She moved somewhere far away — somewhere no one knew her. She had no support system, and she rarely trusted anyone, especially after the baby was born with severe cerebral palsy—retarded and physically disabled.

"Miss Ewa barely scraped together a living as a waitress. She never wanted to take welfare. At a free health clinic, she found a lead on someone to watch Clinton while she worked nights — a kindly grandmother who was long on love but short of cash. Miss Ewa wore out her library card learning about Clinton's condition. She was thoroughly devoted to him—home schooled him even. And if anyone got too nosy about what was wrong with him or wanted to force her to put him in special education, she'd move rather than let them interfere."

In more than an hour-and-a-half of testimony, Mary Ann painted a picture of Ewa Cardy no one ever knew, an Ewa Cardy no one ever bothered to know. It was the picture stitched into her embroidery.

Mary Ann told how Miss Ewa tried to contact her family on many occasions. They continued to reject her for her "shame" and for bringing trouble to the family. Her father blamed her for the rape, saying she must have brought it on herself. She was heartsick when he and her mother took the side of her cousin against her, their own daughter. After numerous tries, she gave up against their cruel and undeserved criticism. It was clear she had been disowned.

"Clinton got very sick in his early twenties," Mary Ann told the jury. "Miss Ewa looked for a doctor. She was careful. Looked out of town in a neighboring community. By then her reputation as a recluse was well established; Clinton's, too, of course. I guess it was how her parents shamed her. She never got out of the shadow of how they turned on her. It was hard for her to live in the light of day. That's partly why she preferred to work nights—also to be with Clinton during his waking hours."

Gifted as a storyteller and wise beyond her years, Mary Ann traced Ewa Cardy's troubles stitch by stitch. She made it simple and direct. Miss Ewa could never have told the story so plainly herself, and the defense never needed her testimony.

"Although she got him medicine and care, it was too late," the girl testified. "He died of pneumonia later at home in her arms. He was the only family she had, and in the end, the only one who really loved her.

"She had no heart to bury him in the cold ground. She didn't have the money to have him cremated either. So she kept his remains in her trunk, and she took him with her wherever she moved. He had been in her cellar here in Azalee for each of the 30 years she's lived here."

The defense attorney was not as taken with the sentimental tale, as was the rest of the teeming courtroom.

"I only have one question," the lawyer said. "If this disabled young man died of natural causes, why did his supposedly devoted mother hide his body for 40 years and throw him out like so much trash after all that time?"

Mary Ann paused — a pause so long that people in the courtroom started shifting in their seats before she resumed her role as the voice of her friend.

"I wondered the same thing myself," she said. "It took me many months to gain the trust of Miss Ewa. I have been her first friend since she was a girl. Maybe because I'm still a girl, it was easier."

"Answer the question," the attorney persisted. "Why would she throw out the body of her son?"

"Our talking helped her with the pain she had bottled up all those years. Eventually, she was ready to let it go—and to let Clinton go."

"But what kind of mother would dump her own son in the trash?" the attorney repeated.

Mary Ann answered with a question: "Who would have believed her the way she has been hated and made fun of in Azalee? It's not like she could walk into the local funeral home or trust anyone to help her bury Clinton. She was afraid of what actually happened—that you'd think she murdered him. If she was ever going to let him go, if she was ever going to escape the awful experiences that ruined her life, hiding him in the trash seemed her best way out. I think she eventually convinced herself that buried is buried, whether in a cemetery or landfill."

The courtroom was silent the rest of the trial, except for the big stir during admission of a DNA report. It confirmed that the body had a 99.99% chance of being Ewa Cardy's son. The dogged defense team even managed to find a nurse, still living, who worked in the health clinic where Miss Ewa took her son for the last time. While no written records still existed, the nurse's testimony was stirring. She described Ewa Cardy's concern about her son. When the clinic never heard from her again, they assumed the boy passed and the mother had moved on, the nurse testified.

Gossip flows incessantly on the grapevine in Azalee. The locals now speculate that Mary Ann Mefford's final appearance on the witness stand and her own unsolicited summation of the case may be what erased any final doubts about Ewa Cardy—what saved her.

"In the end, I think Ewa Cardy taught Azalee a big lesson," Mary Ann admonished the jury. "When she was a young girl, she got pregnant. Her parents threw her out; no one supported her. People in this town imagined all kinds of things about her that weren't true. She lived the story stitched into her crewel embroidery, and it took throwing out her own son for you to see that you did the very same thing to her. You discarded her. "

***

Nearing Christmas a few months after Ewa Cardy's not-guilty verdict, Mary Ann visited Miss Ewa again, bringing some of the Mefford family photo albums.

Ewa gasped when she saw one of the photos.

"Who is that man?" she asked Mary Ann.

"My great grandfather, Nelson Longway."

"Is he still alive?" Miss Ewa asked.

"No, he died some years ago."

The old woman scoured the pages and turned them back and forth, making *tsk-tsk* sounds. She became unusually quiet, and then laughed out loud. Mary Ann had never heard her laugh.

"My dear," Miss Ewa said. "I hope this won't destroy your memory of him, but after all we've been through together, you have to know: your great grandfather was Clinton's father."

Norma Jean **Thornton**

Her baby sister called her Nonie. Her great granddaughter calls her GumGum. Norma Jean Thornton, also known as Noniedoodles and Granny-GumGum, is an art-doodling and writing granny from Rio Linda, California. Her books

include *Nonie's 1ˢᵗ Big Bottom Girls' Rio Linda Cookbook, Noniedoodles, Volumes 1 & 2*, and *Doodle Calendars*.

As Granny-GumGum, she writes children's truth-based animal stories and a variety of fun rhymes.

She blogs at http://NonieDoodles.WordPress.com/Author/NonieDoodles.

She says her other interests can be described as "non-fiction Heinz-57 stuff, dabbling in everyday humor and more rhymes," but her story presented for this book, "The Challenge," is a rare challenging fiction piece based on life-events.

The Challenge

With profound hatred and resentment, Jake stared intently, entirely focused on the object beneath him, for what seemed like forever. Getting a grip on his emotions, he braced for the approaching attack with teeth-gritting fierceness.

He had been hunched over for hours in the same position, both dreading and anticipating this last one with intensity he had never before felt. The first twenty had taken all night, each one seemingly more complicated than the prior. The second twenty had taken all of the next day — again, each one more challenging than the last. The final nineteen had brought him down to this, the most important and most convoluted one, with just an hour left to complete the task.

Jake took a deep breath, held it, and slowly exhaled in an attempt to regain his normal, well-modulated breathing. He had to prevent it from going back to those erratic and harsh spurts of breath that he had experienced, as time drew near this final onslaught.

His shoulders tensed; his back and neck ached. At times his muscles seemed paralyzed, almost frozen. The floor became his prison. His entire body was going on adrenalin, yet his fingers wouldn't cooperate, and his legs stiffened.

Jake's eyes began to blur. He was sweating and felt dizzy. His breath exercises failed; his breathing became shallow and sporadic, even raspy.

He could do this. Just one more to go, then Jake could prove to her that he was capable of anything he had ever told her: how he could do everything so much better, so much quicker.

Jake heard something in the other room, smelled something strong and pungent. Was it her, with some of her "special" coffee? If so, she was early. Had she come back to intimidate him, throw him off his game at the last second to prevent him from succeeding, or had she simply come to gloat, sure in her own mind that he would fail this challenge?

Only fifteen minutes remained until the alarm! Jake was almost ready to taste it, but would it be the bitterness of defeat or the sweetness of success? He had to hurry. Just one more step to go, and it would be all over. Then he could be the one to gloat.

Jake touched the string, and grasped for the scissors, his only weapon during this entire ordeal. At times Jake had even thought of using them on himself, just to be put out of this misery and agony.

Year after year, it was the same thing over and over, Jake chiding her about the time she spent, the complaining she always did. He finally realized how great she had been at it. How had she always managed to do this with such ease and such finesse, even with the grumbling?

Jake felt relief wash over his entire body as he used the scissors to curl the final string.

Done! He had beaten the alarm. The last Christmas present, his wife's, was finally gift-wrapped! Jake had survived the tormenting chore of wrapping all of the presents this year. It was over! His time to gloat!

But only until next Christmas. Then he would willingly and quietly allow his wife that pleasure.

April **Edsberg**

A dventure became a part of April Edsberg's life, when she was four years old. She gave her older brothers her doll buggy wheels for their go-cart. Nestled in safety, with her back against Big Brother, she careened down the hill. Her sacrifice

gave April access to Mr. Epidendio's farm and the blackberry hideout, where she munched on stolen corn, boiled in an army helmet.

When her children were grown, adventure called again. This time, it was an around-the-world trip with her sister. She managed to spend eight months backpacking in the world's most intriguing locations on just $12,000. Her world travel story is packed with laughter, fear, and fascinating people. Look for her book, *Chasing the Sun.*

Circumnavigating Fiji's Mana Island

The sun touches my eyelids, welcoming me to another day in Fiji. I dress in silence and step outside the *mbure*, Fijian hut, shared by ten of us, all backpackers. Before breakfast each morning, I hear the highest hill calling me to climb to its top and count the seventeen uninhabited islands jutting out of the ocean around Mana. The island reassures me that my current situation is not a dream. For years, books about the South Pacific have kept me warm, while my children threw snowballs outside our window. Now I'm here. I'm late, but I'm here!

I feel like loose change sharing an *mbure* with twenty year olds, when I'm fifty-five. We certainly are in different chapters of our lives, viewing this world with different perspectives.

A large rock makes an ideal place to sit and contemplate this world. North, away from the village, parched fields slope down to the blue rollers. No one lives on the steep side.

The village is clumped on the southern shore. Corrugated metal houses stand like an insult to the cobalt sea. What's a person to do? There aren't enough trees to build wooden structures, and the cost to ship wood to this isolated area is prohibitive for islanders.

Two enterprises support the Fijian residences, the Japanese resort and the backpackers.

The short airstrip that separates the island down the middle belongs to the Japanese who lease the west side of the island from the chief. They have an upscale resort, which is dotted with neat, individual bamboo *mbures*.

This side of the runway is the Fijian's world with a dining room for backpackers, and next to that is the church and school with a large playground but no toys.

After a breakfast of fresh mangos, bananas, and toast, I pad down the dirt path from the mbure on the hill to the south and amble east, past the corrugated homes of the village. It's a two- and a half-hour walk around the island, and the snorkeling is supposed to be good at Sunset Beach.

Almost everyone rounds the island to the east, past the resort, to get to Sunset Beach because it is a level path, but I'm wondering what this more rugged route looks like. My expectation of a solitary morning soon evaporates as a scruffy dog joins me. He is about the size of a cocker spaniel, clumped with fur that could have been white at one time. Bathing doesn't seem to be on his schedule. I talk to him as we continue our journey, but can't make myself touch the cruddy pooch. Perhaps, he understands and considers me a fellow traveler.

Two backpackers run up to Scruffy and me, laughing. Becky is about twenty-five years old, and Matt insists he's twenty-two.

Becky slaps her hands together and does a little jig. "I planned to take a two-month holiday before accepting a position in New Zealand, but it has been so much fun that eight months have slipped by. I have rung up Mum twice for more money. Now my savings account is almost empty, so my next stop has to be Wellington, where a job as physiotherapist is waiting for me."

My smile is big. "It's so nice to meet a fellow physical therapist. Guess what? You're the second physiotherapist I've met so far." This walk is going to be more fun than I thought.

The sandy beach is replaced with rough coral as we continue our journey, but Scruffy is still hanging in with us. He likes the stimulation of foreigners. Ahead of us, we see big boulders. At first, we just jump from one to the next, but as they get larger, we have to climb them, which causes Matt to breathe hard. Evidently, hiking isn't his favorite activity.

Tide pools glisten on the ochre ledge, and we stop for a moment to stick a finger into the center of the sea anemones ensconced beneath the clear water. Their little pastel filaments close gently around our finger tickling us as they search for food.

Scruffy and Matt rest in the shade of the cliff as Becky and I walk to the rocky edge and gaze at the distant islands. The shore drops off, and whitecaps whip around near the islands.

The roar of the ocean hitting the precipice ahead of us is audible. I didn't know we'd have to traverse the face of a cliff to get to the beach. It gives me the creeps. What will Scruffy do when we leave him?

Waves slap against the bluff and salt the breeze around us. There are several boulders to scramble over to get to the face of the cliff. Going first is easier for me. Waiting just makes me nervous. My right foot finds a hold, and my toes settle on a little outcrop when Scruffy barks. I twist my body to see if our little dog is sad to be left behind.

Evidently not. Scruffy just jumps into the churning ocean and swims far away from the rocks. I watch as he starts to pass the cliff, swimming to the sandy shore beyond.

He has made this trip before.

Sand sticks to my sweaty hands, and my legs shake. It's just nerves. "Okay, April, take slow, deep breaths." My legs stop rattling. I'm short, and my reach is limited, a flimsy excuse for the knot in my gut. Wouldn't it have been smarter to walk around the other way as sane people do?

The toes of my right foot find a little hole, and I shift my weight. The hold crumbles, and my knee scrapes against the wall. My mind snaps back to my task. My fingers grip tighter, while my foot frantically scrapes along the rocky face in search of stable footing. Sweat drips onto my lips and salts my tongue. Matt and Becky are behind me, so I tighten my gut and continue to edge my way along the cliff. The rhythmic crash of the ocean against the rocks below encourages me to choose my holds carefully. My children still need their mother.

We have worked up a good sweat by the time we hit Sunset Beach, so Matt flops down and grabs a beer from a mate. Scruffy has already ingratiated himself with the group, even though he is soaking wet. I almost feel like petting the tough little guy.

Becky and I don't miss a beat. We slip on our masks and snorkels — no flippers when you backpack — and dive into the water. We're headed northeast toward a light-blue area that we heard was awash with tropical fish.

The tide is fierce, pushing us back to shore. Can we overcome the current? I've never fought the ocean this hard before. Becky hasn't said a word, and I'm not going to bailout first. Within minutes, the sand disappears, and we are over coral covered with slimy seaweed. It's ugly. Depth perception is hard to gauge in the ocean. To avoid getting a cut, I don't stop to tread water.

Ahead we see something blue in the seaweed. We reach it and find royal-blue starfish with thin twelve-inch arms lying on top of the seaweed that covers the coral. Looking at these iridescent starfish as we struggle makes the effort more bearable.

My arms ache as we slowly make progress over the tangled seaweed. The memory of the brilliant starfish dims, as malignant thoughts seep into my head. Even strong swimmers can drown in strong currents, and I'm no competitive swimmer. I lift my head out of the water, but I cannot get high enough to see how much further we have to go to reach the light-colored ocean.

Thirty minutes of fighting the current pass when Becky spits her snorkel out of her mouth and shouts, "Do you want to turn back?"

"No way!" I switch my main effort to my legs to ease my arms. "Enough seaweed. Give me fish!" We struggle on, and by switching from main-effort arms to main-effort legs, I keep a steady pace beside Becky, almost.

Suddenly, the edge drops off, and a "wee" feeling hits my stomach, as if I am starting down a giant roller coaster!

We're fifty feet above the empty sand bottom of a large underwater-canyon! The strong current has dissipated, and myriad brightly colored fish in various shapes waltz around us like a choreographed dance. They wander in and out of the caves on the cliff's wall.

My arms are light now as we gently float. Becky turns onto her back for a rest, and I join her. We need a break.

"April, do you think sharks like this area."

"That's an interesting question." We laugh and continue lying on our backs enjoying the warm water and blue sky. "If a shark comes into this canyon, there is nothing we can do about it." I roll over onto my stomach and join my friend exploring the canyon.

We soar as though we are eagles searching for prey, but it's quiet: no noise of an animal scampering or trees rustling, no howl of the wind whipping through the canyon, no birds to cry out. There is no wall of water to crash against a cliff, nor any waves to wash against a beach. There are no planes to roar overhead, no people in boats, and no people from shore who can see us out here.

A gray flounder, about four-feet in length, comes up to inspect us. He's flat-sided with a roundish silhouette, like a giant nickel, and his little face looks like an old man. He is a friendly guy, who accompanies us for a good fifteen minutes while we dive down to peek into the caves and explore this wild aquarium. We dive. We soar — a fleeting chance to be an eagle.

With reluctance, we swim back to the edge of the canyon and slip into the current, which assists our return to an empty beach. Our exploration took much longer than expected, and now all the backpackers have gone to the dining room for lunch.

Buzzed by our adventure, we grab our towels and buckle on our rubber sandals in silence. In the ocean so long, we walk like sailors, bowlegged and wobbly. Like ancient mariners, we return to land, rich with memories.

Doreen **Beyer**

Doreen Beyer lives in Sacramento with her husband. "Sayonara Yorozu" is her first published work. She is currently at work on a semi-autobiographical book of poetry that threads the narratives of four generations — of grandparents

 from the Philippines lured by Hawaii's sugar industry; of a United States Air Force father stationed in Japan who meets mother, a Japanese national; of growing up (mixed up!) in Hawaii and the mainland, and selective reflections of a younger, multi-ethnic generation. It is a story that will resonate with Asian Americans of mixed parentage and readers with an interest in the effects of cultural values and practices on subsequent generations born in the United States.

Contact her at doreenbeyer13@yahoo.com.

Sayonara Yorozu

Summer 2012.
A rare stop to
Sacramento's Yorozu store
on Riverside Boulevard.
A new interest spurs a search
for rice paper,
the type used in brush painting.
Yorozu is the go-to store
where one can find
obscure oriental items
like white Japanese *tabi*,
the favored foot coverings
worn by gentle, elderly Japanese women
of early childhood memory.
Yorozu reminds me of what
Shirokiya in Honolulu use to be,
before the spill of eateries
and bento boxes
overtook the dry goods
and kitsch.

The store's artificial brightness
fails to waken the sleepy merchandise
nestled contently behind glass cases

or wearily wont to sitting on dust-free shelves.
Silence fills the empty spaces like a shroud.
A large Russian man,
a plain-clothes security guard?
paces the back of the store.
A self-consciousness ebbs
from my casual flow
within the banks of the store's aisles,
passing by origami paper and books,
the varied array of chopsticks and teapots,
Japanese magazines and slippers,
until I stop
at a display of calligraphy brushes
and how-to calligraphy books
carefully arranged on the front counter.

I ask the shrunken man behind the counter,
sitting in a wheelchair,
"Do you have rice paper for brush painting?"
"No."
Absent was the reflexive apology
typical of Japanese merchants.
His laconic response suggests
there are no alternative resources.
Turning to inspect the calligraphy brushes,
I pick one I don't need.
The sticker price,
written in black, permanent ink
reads $7.95
in neat, slanting hand.
I push the brush across the counter.
The old man pulls out a receipt pad and calculator
and in the same careful hand,
writes the day's date,
then totals the amount
and tax owed.

Mid-October 2012.
Today I pay a special visit
to Yorozu.
A handful of cars
park in its lot.
A small handmade sign
near the front entrance announces
everything is 20 percent off.

There is unaccustomed chatter in the store.
Easily a half dozen shoppers browse
and offer comments on the merchandise.
"Didn't mom have this?"
"Do you think Aunt so-and-so still uses this?"
"I've always loved these keychain charms!"

The calligraphy books I regarded
at the last visit,
still sit on the counter.
There are two copies.
I had imagined them gone before today.

The large Russian man cashiers.
No, they are not accepting credit cards yet.
They will be next week.
I ask him if he had been the owner's caregiver.
"No," he says.
He was employed here.
In the store.
"From breakfast until two o'clock."
Another man took
the afternoon shift.
This other man
stayed with the owner
the day he got sick with diarrhea;
an absence that was expected to last

three or four days
until he slipped into a coma
and two weeks later—
he was gone.
He was 93 years old.

Taped to one of the glass double doors
is a recent picture of the owner,
Mr. Eugene Okada.
The half-moon shrug of his shoulders
eclipse his neck,
as hands grip his walker
from extended arms
as he stands,
his waxy pallor a stark contrast
to the tiers of brightly colored key chains
displayed on the counter nearby.

Stepping outside the store,
I admire the deep red rain gutters
that trim the steeped black roof
of the Yorozu store.
It resembles a Japanese temple.
A slice of Japan built at a time
when Japanese Nisei
were reestablishing their communities
and their identities
through things Japanese.
A temple that stood at odds
to the nearby I-80 freeway
and neighboring Target store;
to a diminishing Nisei customer base
and an indifferent Yonsei one.

While the modern world paced furiously
outside Yorozu's glass double doors,
inside,
a quiet, timeless dignity reigned.
Yorozu,
the Japanese general store
and Sacramento landmark
for almost a century,
released its last sigh
on September 21, 2012.

Catherine **Byron**

Catherine Byron a lifelong Montana resident earned her first accolades for writing as an eighth grader. An engraved silver pitcher presented by Prime Minister Nehru, the first prize award for an international writing contest, stands as

evidence of her early passion for writing.

A descendant of two generations of homesteaders, she is actively involved in managing a Montana ranch. Her love of the land and the people, as well as an understanding of the challenges facing the small landowner, make her a voice of the common man.

Falling heir to family papers, journals and letters dating back to the 1880s, Byron's current writing is focused on the Hugh Boyle Incident of 1890, memoirs of her grandparents displaced by the Fort Peck Reservoir, and issues facing rural landowners in 2012. Her work has appeared in Montana newspapers for the last two decades, including the Billings Gazette and Agri News. Visit her website at www.ByronsCorner.com.

Rape Coulee

Rape! The word spreads like wildfire as homesteader visits homesteader up and down the valley flanked by red scoria hills. Fists hit tables and coffee cups jump. Women listen and wrestle down fear.

"Raped her. The bastard. We've all watched him going crazy. Never thought he'd do this."

Men dressed in sweaty work clothes linger and take their conversations outside deliberately out of earshot of the women in the cabins. Toes kick the dusty ground, and heads nod in agreement. A firm handshake and locked eyes pledge action as the visitor departs.

This summer of shame lies hidden for a hundred years. Now locked in a trunk at the back of my dark and dusty attic, my grandmother's hand-scrawled memoirs describe the horror of this closely guarded secret. My search for more information on my maternal ancestors leads me to her scribbled notes. Pouring over the brittle yellow pages, I am speechless when I read her detail of that morning from hell.

Questions clog my mind: Was there a trial? Was there a lynching? Was there a child? Was my grandmother telling the truth? All of it? Part of it? None of it?

I read and reread her faded words. Their content cuts to the core: "July – 1907 – worst day of my life … had my back to the door … scrubbed a tub full of whites … heated more water on the stove … added some lye to break the hardness … heard the door open … thought it was Tom … dirty hand slapped over my mouth … recognized the crazy man's voice … Oh, my God … 'Don't scream or I'll cut your throat!' … waved a knife … trapped … tried to get away … fought, kicked, punched … shoved me onto the bed … tore my clothes … did the unthinkable … left … I begged God to let me die…. bleeding, shuddering, sobbing … seemed like days…"

The only complete sentence in her whole story is a prayer to die. My head spins! Suddenly my mother's birthplace raises a flood of questions. Whose blood courses through my veins? Who was the father of mother's dead baby sister? Why does no one ever speak of the tiny grave out at the coast?

Digging through homestead patents, I uncover the names of the homesteaders in that century-old community. I pour over topographic maps. Then it jumps off the page into my throat: Rape Coulee! Oh my God! Can it be? Could it be? My heart pounds and my knees go weak.

Township, range, and section: carefully I draw an outline of the holdings on my landowner map. "Mr. Reilly." The unfamiliar name is listed as the holder of the deed. I stop at a local hardware store and ask if the owner knows him. "He doesn't come in very often," the clerk says. "His hired man is the one we see. Reilly is a newcomer. He bought the place after old-man Hadley died about five years ago. From what I've heard and seen, even though he's new here, he's sure he knows most of the local history. Sometimes he has it straight, but from what I've heard, more often he doesn't know what he's talking about." A new customer walks through the door ending our conversation.

My finger slides down the small print in the phone book. There it is: Reilly. I punch the number into my cell phone. "Hello." His

greeting sounds as if he is closing a conversation rather than invit-
ing one!

"Hello, Mr. Reilly, I'm working on some family research and am
interested in a homestead site on Township 4, Range 27, Section
11. According to the maps I have, that is land you own."

All is silent on the other end. "Is there a chance that I could come
out and get to that site? I have a four-wheel drive."

Clearing his throat, he answers, "When can you come? I'll be
around tomorrow and the next day. I'll drive you up there. Could
you be here right after lunch?"

My heart sings! Carefully I prepare for this trip. Maps, my GPS,
and a camera fill my duffle bag. On the drive up the narrow valley, I imagine wagons and teams trailing through the shadows of
these red hills a century ago. Suddenly, there it is. Reilly. The name
is professionally painted on a shiny black mailbox. I slow and turn
into the driveway.

A red Dodge Ram dually is parked in the yard. If this is Reilly's
outfit, it hasn't seen much ranch use. The front door opens, and a
tall slender dude steps onto the porch. Exiting my car to greet him,
I carry the map rolled up under my arm. After brief introductions,
I unroll the map across the hood of the red pickup. Together our
fingers trace the route to the cabin site abandoned a century before, noting the names on patents issued to the neighboring homesteaders along the way.

Mischievously I test the depth of his local history knowledge:
"How on earth did this coulee get this name?" I plant my finger
under the bold label on Rape Coulee. Trying to conceal my keen
interest, I await his answer.

"Don't know. I have no idea."

My heart rejoices! I feel safe. My cover is not blown.

Confused by my reaction, I begin to ponder. Am I assuming the
shame of that dastardly act 100 years before? And why would I

do so? Emotions erupting like Fourth of July fireworks course through my being. It must be shame. Why else would I be relieved by the man's ignorance? We bounce over sagebrush and cactus all the while hugging the side of the creek. Dust and the scent of sage fill the cab. We do not speak. Twenty minutes later, he stops. "This is it."

Here it is — the site of my grandparents' honeymoon cottage. They built it together, nestled into a timbered cove in that drainage. Rape Coulee! The name sends shivers down my spine, then nausea, fleeting but intense.

At the site, we find a sandstone foundation, now crumbled. A rusted bucket, an old door hinge, and a brown medicine bottle jut out of the cut bank. Probably their middens, I think, wishing for more time to dig. I walk around and snap pictures. I take a GPS location and frantically jot notes. "Possible chicken coop here, cow barn there." I sketch what seems an outline of a corral onto a crude map, writing, "House clearly concealed from view. Door probably on the east side, very hidden by the hill."

My silence cranks up the volume of the chatterbox landowner. "So what d'ya know about these people? Where'd they go from here? They prove up or just leave? They go broke? What were their names again?"

"Burlington," I say through my distraction. "Tom and Katie Burlington."

"Never heard of 'em." He goes into a monologue about the struggles of homesteaders and how so many were not prepared the meet the challenges of hard work and primitive living.

Tuning out the sound of Reilly's voice, my soul drinks in the warmth of the sun on my back, the sounds of the wind, the birds, the hoppers, and the frogs. It is as though one sits in the lap of Mother Nature in this place. What horror could have pierced this silence and reverie? What degree of horror does it take to carve a name on a map that endures for more than a century?

Standing for one last look as Reilly checks his watch again then opens the pickup door to leave, I ask myself, "Do I have the courage to dig up the full truth of this story?" Then it strikes me. Digging up the truth is one thing. Having the guts to write it in what may become a twisted family tree is quite another.

Laurie **Hoirup**

L aurie Hoirup is the retired chief deputy director for the California State Council on Developmental Disabilities. Now fifty-seven, she has lived with a significant physical disability since the age of two, using a wheelchair since the age of

 five. She is diagnosed with spinal muscular atrophy (SMA 2).

She lives in Sacramento with her husband. She is a mother of two adult children and a grandmother of three grandsons.

Her memoir *I Can Dance: My Life with the Disability* is her first book, adding to her writing contributions found on Internet websites.

Learn more about her story and see pictures of her growing up at www.LauriesLegacy.com.

My Husband, a Caregiver

The term caregiver carries some stodgy definitions. A caregiver looks after another. The job description can include principal responsibility for the welfare of children, the innumerable needs of dependent adults and the convalescence of ill and disabled persons.

These definitions create clear images, varying from a parent caring for their own child, a nurse caring for their patients, a spouse caring for their ailing life's partner, and an adult child caring for their aging parents. In many cases, the definition also conjures pictures of a friend caring for another dear friend in need.

For most people, these images include an assumed, finite time period. The parent raises a child for eighteen years. An aging parent may need care for ten to fifteen years on average. A career in caregiving can last thirty years, five days a week for eight hours a day.

Whatever the scenario, caregivers usually take time for their own personal lives to offset the enormous demands of serving others. The parents enjoy their marriage or find diversion in their careers. Children go to school for a major part of the day and give their parents a respite. Nurses work at their job only for a portion of each day, and then their shifts end. A spouse who cares for an ailing partner generally does not face this situation until much later in life, as it is with the care of an aging parent.

I preface my story with these definitions and situations because my caregiver has devoted the majority of his life to the care of others — not for a finite time period, but for ongoing and constant care, the kind that involves more than thirty years, often seven days a week and twenty-four hours a day. It is a gift of service that represents the definition of caregiver like no other.

My caregiver is also my husband. Unlike other spouses who care for an ailing partner later in life, my husband started out as my caregiver from the beginning of our relationship. I have had a disability my entire life. However, my husband's caregiving career began long before we met, some thirty years ago.

My husband's name is JR. He began his caregiving career as a medic upon completion of diving school. As a professional diver, he worked the speedboat racing circuit as a rescue diver saving those injured during accidents. Later he returned to college and began care for students with disabilities. That led to more work caring for the elderly as well.

What started out as a part-time job quickly evolved into a live-in job because most people with significant disabilities find it difficult to maintain several people around the clock as caregivers. JR quickly became friends with the people he served and he is still friends with many of them today.

Experience taught him about more and more types of disabilities. He often traveled across country, turning to caregiving as a means of support, but he never lost sight of his responsibility to the people he cared for.

This career path led JR into my life. I have been a wheelchair user since the age of five. Quadriplegia renders me incapable of taking care of any of my own personal needs. I had been married, divorced, and living as a single mom with two children, ages eight and four, when JR first answered my ad for a caregiver. I felt blessed when I met this man. He came with references singing his praises. They expressed admiration for his giving and responsible nature.

His willingness to care for my children, as well as myself, led me to feel as though I had died and gone to heaven. Anyone relying on another individual to make their life work understands why these attributes are so earth shattering and what type of person it takes to do this kind of job.

Obviously, our lives took another direction as we grew closer together. We eventually fell in love and married. JR became my full-time caregiver. He chose to continue his role in my daily care because it simply worked for our lives. He helped me to raise my children (our children), while at the same time supporting me through college. During this stage of his life, he was not only caregiver to me, but also to the children.

Once the children were grown, we considered hiring someone else, but for the time being, this situation continued to be the best fit for us because my own career was advancing. The governor appointed me chief deputy director for a disability agency. JR enabled me to fulfill my many job duties, involving out-of-town travel, long hours, and weekends. He also provided me with the assurance of getting to work on time, and he played the perfect host for all the entertaining we did around my job.

More specifically, JR took care of all my personal care: showering, grooming, dressing, feeding, and toileting — everything except my makeup. He took care of all of the domestic chores: cooking, cleaning, laundry, and shopping, and he still found time to engage in the regular husband-type duties: handyman tasks, automobile repair, yard work and pets.

Somehow, he managed to find time to exercise and keep in shape. Putting this all down on paper makes me wonder how he did it all. He truly is amazing! What is most remarkable about him is, through it all, he remained romantic and loving, always making time for us. He is truly my husband/soulmate first, my best friend second and last, but not least, my caregiver.

You might think the story ends here, but there is one additional piece to add. About twelve years ago, his ninety-five-year-old grandmother from Canada was stricken with Alzheimer's. After several years of sharing the responsibility of watching over her, none of his other family members could continue to take her in and provide the care she needed. JR and I both felt strongly that a nursing home was not the answer, so we invited her to live with us.

Since JR was already home caring for me and I went to work each day, he felt he would be able to take care of his grandmother as well. The situation did require some relief by another caregiver for a few hours, so he could continue to run our home, but for the most part, he was her sole caregiver, as he was mine.

For a year or two, while I worked in Southern California, JR actually had a few hours every day to play and do the things he wanted to do for himself. Soon we relocated to a new town, found a new home, took on a new job, and added new responsibilities. With his grandmother living with us, he found that caregiving once again replaced his personal time.

Sadly, his grandmother passed away, giving JR some more personal time, but not for long. Within two years, my health took a nosedive, and I had no choice but to retire. Even with JR's devoted assistance, I could not keep up with the rigorous demands of my position. My needs required full-time care.

We have recently hired someone to assist in the mornings through early afternoon, but JR can never be too far away. I still need him to assist with the many areas of my care too difficult for my attendant. Of course, he is still my primary caregiver afternoons, evenings, and weekends.

As you can plainly see, JR's caregiving began in his early twenties by choice, as a form of employment first, but eventually as a responsibility for friends and family. He did not set out to fall in love with someone who was going to need a caregiver for her entire life, but it happened. He never dreamed he would be his grandmother's caregiver, but it happened as well.

So it would appear that other than during childhood and adolescence, JR is a lifetime caregiver, covering all the scenarios listed in my introduction: caregiver to children, friends, patients, spouse and grandparent. Through it all, he remained loving and supportive, always putting others before himself.

For this reason, I believe he should be acknowledged, and this is my way of doing just that. He has touched so many people's lives and made them better for no real personal gain. I would love to see him take some time just for himself (although I am sure he would probably include me). I wish there were an award that could allow him to do that, but absent that reality, my love for him will have to suffice. This is my husband's caregiving story with no end in sight.

Tom**Kando**

Tom Kando, PhD, grew up in World War II Europe, spending his formative years in Paris and Amsterdam. At eighteen, he came to America as a lonely immigrant and a Fulbright student. He became a professor at major universities, taught in

prisons, and lectured worldwide. His memoir, *A Tale of Survival,* describes his far-flung and sometimes harrowing experiences.

He authored articles about crime, terrorism, psychology, sports, and travel in the *Wall Street Journal,* the *Los Angeles Examiner* and other venues, and nine books, including *Leisure and Popular Culture, Social Interaction* (C.V. Mosby), *Sexual Behavior and Family Life* (Elsevier), and *Readings in Criminology* (Kendall Hunt).

In his short story, "Absolution," Kando deals with love, loneliness, guilt, paranoia, brainwashing, and other often-disturbing psychological phenomena.

He lives in Gold River, California. His website is www.TomKando.com.

Absolution

It was Matt's first invitation since he moved to the city. He did not feel much like going. He didn't usually enjoy parties — he assumed that the invitation was for a party — least of all those superficial social events organized by some club. Judging from the invitation they sent, it was bound to be one of those boring, alcohol-free affairs. However, he was in no position to be picky. He had no friends in this new town, and this might be the opportunity to meet new people. Indifferent, he decided to go.

As usual, while driving to the party, he could not stop himself from building expectations. His usual fantasies overtook him: pictures of wild happenings with luscious girls. One of them would go home with him well before the end of the party.

He realized that his trend of thought was dysfunctional. It undoubtedly would lead to disappointment. In fact, his imagination caused him to lose track of his route. Absorbed in his imagery, he ended up in an utterly unfamiliar part of town. He reached the given address only after several errors, consultation with gas station attendants, and an exhaustive appeal to a cop.

He arrived several hours late, wondering if the event might be over by now. Judging from outside — the old wooden building was barely lit up, and there were few cars in front — the party was either over or not successful.

The outer door was unlocked, so he went right in. He followed signs with arrows and the instructions, "COME UP. YOU ARE LATE!" He realized that he had badly misjudged the size of the building from the outside. He walked past half a dozen such signs, down a number of hallways, and up and down several flights of stairs before eventually finding himself in front of a closed door. He assumed that this was the entrance to the party. Disoriented, he could not remember in what part of the building he was. For all he knew, this well could be underground.

He knocked on the door, and it opened immediately.

"Mack!" he said.

This was truly incredible. He hadn't seen Mack in at least eight years, and he had no idea that man was in town, in this new and unwelcome metropolis where he himself seemed a pilgrim. Frankly, he never liked Mack much. They went to school together. Mack was about four years older and a Lampwick. He had introduced Matt to certain aspects of the big life — women, smoking, drinking — and he had also cheated him on several occasions. No, Matt certainly was not happy to see this so-called friend. Confused and somewhat anxious, he asked, "Mack, why...what the devil are you doing here?"

Mack's physiognomy had not changed. His rotund face still seemed ageless, and sarcasm remained a permanent feature of his expression. He smiled and said, "We'll discuss that later, Matt. Right now, let's focus on you. Come on in; make yourself at home."

Still baffled by this unexpected reunion, Matt apologized for being late.

"That's alright, we knew you'd be late," Mack answered.

"We?" Matt asked. "Are *you* giving this party?"

"Yes, me and all these other folks. Go meet them. I'm sure you'll find them fascinating."

Matt walked into the next room. He found it darker and crowded.

The light was reddish, suitable for printmaking in a darkroom. The background music consisted of a soft drumbeat, undergirding a jazzed-up electronic rendition of Shostakovich's second waltz. He approached a small group gathered in a corner. They turned toward him, and Matt heard a tall old man say, "Ah, Mr. Matthew, we've been waiting for you; you are late."

Taken back, Matt said that he was sorry to arrive so late, but his curious thoughts muffled his words. *Who were these people, anyway? Why did they say that they had been waiting for me?* He started again.

"Well you see," he explained, "I got lost on my way over. I am not familiar with this city—"

"I see," one of them said. "You are new here?"

"Yes, I've only been here for a few months."

"A few months?" another chimed in. "Surely you should be familiar with the city by now."

Ignoring the rude rebuke, Matt countered that some of the neighborhoods still confused him, especially at night.

"He gets confused at night," said the tall old fellow who had been the first to criticize him. The whole group snickered.

What is this? Matt wondered. *Why are these people mocking me?* He excused himself, walked to the bar, and poured himself a glass of Cabernet. Fortunately, the party was not dry as he had feared.

As he was pouring the wine into his glass, a woman approached him. She acted important, wearing a shiny embroidered dress and lavish jewelry. She coifed her phony platinum hair into a convoluted beehive. Her middle age matched her middle weight.

"I see that you're making abundant use of our resources, Mr. Matthew," she said, sarcastic and accusatory.

Matt was flabbergasted once again. *Does everyone here know who I am? And is everyone equally rude?*

Pent up in confusion, he considered telling her to go to hell; instead, he apologized. "Oh, yes, well…forgive me; I forgot to bring my own. But I'll be glad to pay if this is a no-host—"

"Never mind," she said dismissively. "Next time you should ask for permission to buy a drink, and please don't serve yourself."

"I understand," Matt replied, trying to smile. "Thank you so much. I can certainly use a glass of wine. You know what they say about wine being a social lubricant or something."

"A *what?*" the matronly woman said, disgust contorting her face. "Are you a pervert? I won't tolerate such language in my house!"

Jeez! Matt thought. *Must everything go wrong tonight? Now what did I do?*

"Alright," he admitted, "I realize my choice of words wasn't great. Anyway, I'm sorry about the wine, and I'm returning it to you right now," whereupon he replaced his untouched glass on the bar.

This did not placate the apparent hostess. She said, "Don't try to back-pedal, mister! The damage is done. Others will suffer the consequences of your thoughtlessness as they always have. And by returning the wine you poured into your glass, you are signaling you don't like it."

Confused, Matt replied, "I'm sure that this is a fine wine, but I don't want to abuse your hospitality."

"A fine wine?" she asked aggressively. "You haven't even tasted it. You take me for a fool?"

Every word Matt uttered worked against him. He felt more and more muddled. But because he was a guest, after all, he bit his tongue once more. Instead of telling the woman to go fuck herself, he said, "Well, what I mean is…I'm sure you serve fine wines, but since you said that the supply is limited, I thought—"

"Limited?" she exclaimed in a shrill voice. "Are you accusing me of being limited?"

"No, not at all," Matt said nervously. "I just meant…uh…"

By now Matt's "conversation" with this woman had become loud.

A crowd gathered. Turning to some of the bystanders, the matron said, "Hey guys, you know what Matt here thinks of us? He feels that we're 'limited'!"

"Is that so?" someone said. "We thought that tonight's focus would be on *his own* limitations."

"Yes," continued the hostess, "and we are certainly aware of your limitations, Mr. Matthew! As well as your *motives*."

My motives? Matt thought. *What on earth are they talking about? What do they know about me?*

The growing group surrounding Matt now also included the first guests with whom he had tangled after he arrived. For a moment, the silence grew ominous. The tall old man who had berated Matt for being late said, "We know a lot about you, young man. Don't try to deceive us."

"Yes," added a shadowy figure, "he's already admitted that he gets confused at night — *timor nocturnia!*"

"Confused?" another shouted. "He is probably just *malingering*, not confused!"

"Maybe you're right," said the group's ringleader, then turning to Matt. "Admit what *really* happened, Mr. Matthew. Don't try to evade the issue."

The group stood around him in silence, a sinister smile on its collective face. Matt's embarrassment turned into fear and anger. *Who are these Bozos?* he wondered. *What right do they have to treat me like this?* He wanted to leave, but he did not want to create a scene. After all, they had been kind enough to invite him. So he put his best foot forward and feigned an accommodating smile.

"Well, it's true that I was distracted while coming over, and that's why I got lost," he admitted.

"Aha!" said the tall old guy, always ready to pounce. "I knew it!" Then he asked, "What were you thinking about?"

"I don't remember," Matt replied.

"You're lying, Mr. Matthew," he countered. "You're not doing your best. We know what you were thinking about!"

Matt's anger grew. "What are you insinuating?" he demanded. "What right do you have to treat me like this?"

"What right? You came to us, didn't you?" he retorted. "We know why you came, and it's too late to turn back now."

Matt's anger made space for fear. *What did they know about him?* he wondered. *And who had told them?*

"Yes," the ringleader continued. "We know the truth. This is your last chance."

"Last chance for what?" Matt asked, approaching panic.

"The last chance for you to face the truth."

"I see," Matt said, but he did not see. *What did they mean by truth? Did they know some deep dark secret in his subconscious? Some skeleton in the closet he was unaware of? What* truth *did they have in mind? What is* truth *anyway?*

"The truth?" he equivocated. "Aren't there many truths?"

Isn't that what postmodernists say? Have you read Baudrillard, or Derida? Postmodernists stress the multiplicity of narratives. And modern cosmology teaches us that."

This only made things worse. The youngest in the group interrupted him forcefully, "You're full of shit, Matthew. We're all aware of your mystifications. Solipsism will not save you!"

The others laughed

"Truth is in the *mind!*" the youngest said.

This triggered a flood of thoughts in Matt's mind — *bad faith, false consciousness, mental dishonesty. Were they talking about that? Is that why they were all mad at him? Maybe they had a point. Maybe he was guilty. He certainly felt increasingly guilty. After all, they all appeared to agree about his guilt. Surely, they couldn't all be wrong, could they?*

He wanted to convince them he was not bad. His greatest desire was no longer to leave, but to win their friendship and their acceptance. *If I only could make them like me again*, he thought. *If I confess, they will be nice to me.*

"Alright," he admitted, "maybe I've made some mistakes. Maybe we started on the wrong foot, but I'm willing to learn."

The woman who had reprimanded him earlier addressed the group, "Only Schmul can help him now. He is too far gone!" She instructed Mack to fetch Schmul — whoever he was.

* * *

The wait for Schmul was intense. When he arrived, the mystery man was in the company of a retinue that included Mack and a couple of others. The cortege signaled Schmul as the big Kahuna. He was mid-sized and middle-aged. He stood with a balding cranium, a mustache and a thick black beard. He wore a long, light-colored mantle. As he approached Matt, solemnly he said, "I hear that you are in trouble. We will help you."

"Yes, Schmul," said Mack reverently. "He is *mens improbum*. The curriculum applies."

Matt felt his remnant of self-control slipping away. His mind struggled against him. *Who was Schmul? And what was Mack saying?* In a supreme effort at rationality, he turned toward Schmul and said, "What are you going to do to me? I only came here because I was invited — I guess by my old friend Mack."

"I am not his friend," Mack shouted to the group, "*Mens improbum* lies."

"Yes," a sycophant added. "And his answers are wrong."

Schmul held up his hand solemnly. Total silence descended on the group. Then, he pronounced his plan of action: "We shall help him."

He grabbed Matt by the arm and pulled him into a large adjacent circular hall, which Matt had not yet seen. The group followed. They joined a sizeable crowd already present. After entering, Matt began to recognize some familiar faces, many of which he had not seen in years.

Everybody looked melancholic. Festive talk subsided. Whispers faded into the walls. Even the low-level murmur stopped when Matt was shoved forcefully to the middle of the hall. The crowd turned toward him and receded silently against the wall, forming a threatening circle.

Matt had stumbled to the floor. He had difficulty getting up. Looking at the dozens of faces surrounding him, he realized escape was impossible. Schmul walked around him four times and then broke the silence. Addressing the crowd in a loud, commanding voice, he said, "Here he is, my friends. We have all been waiting for him. We forgave him and offered him reconciliation. We warned him and gave him his chances. Yet, as you can see, he has not repented. He is still in *selfstasis*. He cannot fuse—"

"Please, "Matt interrupted in a final fumbling effort. "I repent. I swear it. I thank you for discovering my guilt, I confess, and I apologize. I will leave in shame, and I will never return."

Indignation rose from the multitude. Amid gasps, Schmul said, "You see, friends, even now the disease progresses. What is your verdict?"

"Help him! Help him! Help him! Help him!" the crowd roared in unison.

Schmul turned to Matt and spoke seriously, "Matt, it is our undivided decision that we shall help you. Come with me."

Schmul and two of his acolytes pulled Matt away toward one of the round room's dark exits. Matt anticipated the sentence about to be delivered. It was the horror of rejection, the terror of being alone. He turned to the crowd and begged, "Please don't put me out! Please let me stay! I love you! I want to be your friend. I want to be like you!"

Schmul ordered his acolytes to bring Matt back to the middle of the room. "Undress," he ordered.

Matt obeyed. He stood naked and shivering. The crowd exploded in laughter. Matt looked down in silence. Finally, Schmul tossed some clothes to him and told him to cover up.

"Oh, thank you!" Matt exclaimed, tears pouring down his cheeks. "Thank you so much! You have saved me!"

As if by rote, Schmul ordered a large hirsute man to walk over to Matt. The hulking man gave Matt a big bear hug.

Matt accepted this ritual passively. Buried in the huge man's embrace, he could smell the stench of his breath, his sweat, and his body. Then a wrinkled and toothless old woman joined them and kissed Matt all over his face. Soon the crowd joined in, forming a mountain of people, hugging, and caressing Matt and each other, Matt buried at the core.

Schmul segregated himself from the human pile, lotus position. "Do we love him?" he shouted.

The group responded with a loud, monosyllabic, "LOVE!" They continued the chant until it muffled into mumbling.

Little by little, people began to fall away. Some left the room. Others reposed on couches or sprawled on the floor. Each began to fall asleep, some in sleeping bags, a few exposed to the emptiness of a party gone cold.

The chanting had a curiously soporific effect on Matt. He could not keep his eyes open. Just before he fell asleep, he thought, *They love me now. They have forgiven me. I am saved. I will never be alone again.*

Linda **Menicucci**

Linda D. Menicucci, Ph.D., is a licensed clinical psychologist. She practiced for many years in San Francisco, specializing in children, families, women, and dream analysis.

She was a California State Fellow in psychology

 and on the medical staff of St. Mary's Hospital and the faculty of the University of California at San Francisco. She also served as a court-appointed expert witness in child psychology. She studied Jungian psychology at the Jung Institute in both San Francisco and Zurich, Switzerland.

In 2001 she moved to Paradise, California, to pursue writing. Her memoir pieces about her Italian family and growing up in the 1960s have won several awards.

She is presently at work on a collection of essays titled *Words That Can Change Your Life.*

Legacy

How do we learn about love? We learn by what we see around us. This is a story about what I saw.

My mother, Dolores, had three sisters. Pasqualina, known as Bessie, was the eldest. A midwife delivered her on January 14, 1900, in Queens, New York. She was the first of twenty-one children; only six survived to adulthood. When Bessie turned twenty-three, her mother died, worn out by illness, childbirth, and miscarriages, leaving Bessie to raise the youngest three children: Julie, aged nine; Dolores, six; and Carmine, four.

Bessie was the only mother these three would remember over their long lives and they remained devoted to her, and she to them. Mary and Johnny, the older two children, were already on their own.

When I was born, Bessie had already turned fifty. She had snow-white hair and a patrician profile, like those found on ancient Roman coins. She and her sisters were slight of build. Like many of their era, they never reached five feet. But this lack of height indicated no lack of stamina. They went to work when they were twelve, and none of them retired before seventy. They lived together through the Depression, working at both a paper bag plant and a shirt factory.

In the late 1930s, Julie married and moved away. When her marriage failed a few years later, she returned to Bessie, Dolores, and their father. Between the three women, they were able to take care of each other, their father — blinded by glaucoma — and Julie's baby son.

During World War II, times turned better. The workforce needed women, and the sisters worked at better paying jobs, Bessie at Greenpoint Hospital, Dolores at the St. Moritz Hotel, and Julie in an office. Dolores married after the war and moved into an apartment downstairs from her sisters. When my mother, Dolores, my father, and I moved to San Francisco from Brooklyn in 1954, Bessie and Julie followed.

During my childhood, we lived only a few blocks from my two aunts. We went over to their house on Sundays to visit. They were the only family I knew. They could talk for hours with no let up about the past, the present, or the future. Any topic proved fair game. They would discuss presidents, the English Royals, the news, and stories that had taken place before I was born.

Julie and Dolores frequently would ask Bessie to tell them about "Mama." Bessie would say, "Mama was beautiful. She had chestnut hair and dark brown eyes. Papa called her his 'Rose.' Mama was a lady. She never went out without her hat and gloves, even when she was sick. The doctor who came to the house loved Mama and loved her cooking."

Bessie would cook and present the food to her sisters. In turn, they would ooh and aah over stuffed bell peppers, minestrone soup, pasta and beans, sausage and peppers, and Italian cake that only she could make. Bessie used no written recipes, so nothing tasted the same twice. They would laugh, fight, argue, and eat for hours around the Formica kitchen table. When they did not want me to understand, they spoke Italian. They never tired of each other, and I never tired of them. When I married and had my own family, I brought them over on Sundays and for every special occasion, I cooked for them, and they would ooh and aah for me.

When Bessie turned eighty she needed a pacemaker to keep her heart beating regularly. Before the surgery, she let everyone know she was "going home," a prospect that pleased her immensely. She thought eighty years were enough to put into her existence. When the surgery went well, Bessie became upset, claiming it was evidence God didn't want her.

Her reaction to God's rejection was marriage. Ralph was eighty-five and six-foot-two. He had spent more than forty years as a merchant marine. He loved Bessie's petite size, her cooking, and her demure lady-like ways. She always stood ramrod straight and sat with her hands folded. She never, in my memory, crossed her legs, even at the ankle.

Bessie had been married once before at age forty, but the man turned out to be a bigamist. My aunt never became aware of this until the funeral. She got the bill, and the first wife got the pension.

At ninety, Bessie learned her pacemaker battery needed replace-ment. Again, she anticipated her earthly release, but God remained unavailable. Soon after, Ralph died, and by ninety-five, Bessie suf-fered a stroke that made her unable to care for herself.

Her two sisters, now eighty-one and seventy-eight, could not care for her. Bessie spent the next five years in a nursing home.

Julie and Dolores moved into an apartment building next to the residence, so they could visit Bessie every day. They would sit to-gether on the outside patio for hours. I would bring them cannoli, their favorite Italian dessert, and they would eat, laugh, and talk. I watched as Bessie's eyes began to dim over these years. Her spirit, unbowed by almost one hundred years of living, began to with-draw. But Julie died first on a November day at age eighty-four from heart failure. The staff of the nursing home and my mother decided it would be in Bessie's best interest not to reveal that her sister had died.

One year later, two events converged. Bessie asked me if Julie had died, and I said yes. That same week, the doctors decided not to replace Bessie's pacemaker. She was too frail at ninety-nine years of age. Three days later, Bessie died in her sleep, one year after her sister Julie died and two months short of her hundredth birthday.

As if in sequence, my mother, Dolores, saw her health decline. She now needed assistance in living. At eighty-two, her body had shrunk to eighty pounds, and she could no longer walk. I could not tell her about Bessie.

Christmas came and went. In mid-January, my mother began to reveal conversations she said she exchanged with Bessie. She explained that Bessie called her to come upstairs where my mother, Dolores, would be happier. She said Bessie told her that there was no pain where she was now and that everyone was waiting for her. My mother's hearing had been significantly impaired since her near death in the 1917 influenza epidemic that killed millions worldwide. When I asked her why I couldn't hear Bessie, she said my ears weren't open yet. My mother decided to do what her sister wanted. Soon after our conversation, she went to bed and slipped into a coma. She died two weeks later on January 20, 2000, two months to the day after Bessie.

I have been a psychologist for thirty years. I have seen tragedy, heartbreak, joy, and forgiveness. I have seen death and new life, both in a child born and in a spirit reborn. But the most powerful lesson I have learned came from these three sisters. Love has no boundary. It speaks to us from beyond this existence, if only we have the ears to hear.

Matthias **Mendezona**

Matthias Mendezona is the author of *How Sweet The Mango, No?: The Journey of a Hispanic Amerasian,* a story that depicts the universal struggles of a man, his land, conflicting identities and true heritage.

Matthias was born to a Basque father and a Filipino-American mother in the island of Mindanao, Philippines. Jesuit-educated, he grew up on a coconut farm with a jungle at the back of the house and the beach up front, spending much of his childhood summers with his American grandfather who taught him about the tropical jungle, wildlife, and interacting with the ethnic tribe called the Subano.

Matthias immersed himself in the business, social, and economic life of the Philippines, participating actively in that nation's search for its own identity. He holds a master's degree in management and an undergraduate bachelor's degree in the behavioral sciences.

Music Blends

The Moorish music, the Spanish guitar,
the gypsy rhythms blend together.
Yet the tune is Marvin Gaye's.
In staccato now, then in soft flowing notes.
The drums enter, and the guitar's bass
marches time with light and high string guitar tones.
What sounds from centuries gone by?
Whence did they come? How did they arrive at this place
in harmony for us to hear?
What depths and beats and homes and kingdoms
brought forth this beauty?
What wisdom has this music created
that we may for the moment
forget the differences and violence we inflict
one to another in the name of other gods?
Praise be the music.
Praise be the bonds that remind us all
how we are one.

Vicki **Ward**

Vicki Ward is passionate about her seasoned view of life and is, herself, a Seasoned Sistah, focusing her research on maturing women's aging and lifestyle concerns.

Her award-winning books affirm the powerful  bonding effect of women sharing affirming life stories and the benefits of strengthening bonds between women. She authored *Savvy Sassy and Bold After 60, A Midlife Rebirth,* a handbook for maturing women packed with vital strategic tips to assist them in making midlife health, financial, and lifestyle decisions. She edited *Life's Spices from Seasoned Sistahs,* a collection of life stories reviewed as *"a book with sassiness and covered with wisdom gained from living."*

As a retired Seasoned Sistah, she observes life, from a mature perspective, writes and publishes books in Brentwood California. Visit her website at www.NubianImagesPublishing.com.

My New White Bucks

My friends and I could not wait to get back to school. After all, sixth grade was, according to everything we had learned from Margaret's and Debbie's older sisters, the time when we became young women.

As the first day of school crept closer, my friends and I made entering school as sixth-graders our only concern, filling all our conversation. We exchanged ideas, girlish ideas and thoughts about how much older we were. We confessed to each other which boys we thought were cute and which were not — until we moved on, piling up a mountain of ideas about the new clothes we had purchased.

On that first day of school, I wore a new red and green plaid skirt, a white blouse and white socks. This skirt set was a big seller in 1960. Highlighting my back-to-school outfit was my new pair of white bucks, accompanied by an accessory that captured all my thoughts.

For some reason — and I don't know why — I held this one accessory back from the group. I don't remember having a conscious thought about what I was going to do. It just felt like I was doing something for me, not just for the girls, something that I felt special about. I just knew in the days before school opened, I wanted to make an impression!

Once I held back the secret article, I knew I had something different from any of the *Gibbs Girls,* even though I was without any plan about what I would do with it. Gibbs Avenue is the street we all grew up on, where adornments were scarce. Later grown up, the five of us would identify ourselves with that avenue, where we came of age — the Gibbs Street Housing Projects in Alameda, California, in the early 1960s.

The post-World-War-II era housing projects sat adjacent to the fully commissioned Alameda Naval Air Station. The base was the reason many of our parents had planted roots there; they were dependent families of men serving their tour of duty stationed to the naval base.

Yes, military housing was available. But it required months of waiting and living in temporary housing — or the "projects" as they were more affectionately known. Many of the military families took advantage of the preferred living conditions on base. Conversely, for other families, the housing offered on base still proved too costly, and the projects became a cost-effective way of providing shelter for their burgeoning families.

For many non-military families, the projects represented affordable housing for couples with families who had migrated west from the Deep South in search of better jobs for themselves and educational opportunities for their children. Often hearing from family and friends that jobs were available, they followed others, building a close community of related families, friends, and acquaintances.

Many residents lived at or below the poverty level. Money was scarce for most families, and our household was no exception. We became accustomed to the basics. Occasionally we got something special. We were fortunate that both parents worked, so we had a car.

I found it unusual that mom was going to drive us to Hales Department store in Oakland to get school clothes. Although it was a short trip through the Posey Tube, a connecting underwater tunnel, it was a new experience. When I asked my mom, she told me we'd find more shopping opportunities than we had available on our tiny island.

Little did she or I realize that the shopping trip would a catalyst for changes that were to begin in me. The excursion to Oakland taught me something new about myself. I began to see myself differently. Maybe my friends' older sisters were right.

As the new day approached, we talked incessantly, endlessly, about entering sixth grade at Longfellow Elementary School. What would it mean for us? What could we expect? We were ready to find out. So the Gibbs Girls agreed to leave early for the first day of school. We wanted to get there early to see everything, whatever that was.

Margaret was the first to get to my house. I knew it was her, and I ran to open the door. Immediately the mixed squeals went up. I quickly pushed her back onto the porch and hopped out, pulling the door shut behind me. I had to act fast because I knew my mom would shout for us to hush up. We looked each other up and down. We let out more squeals, signaling our pleasure with each other's outfit. We took turns twirling around, posing, and showing off either a skirt or a blouse, commenting on colors, socks, and hair.

I watched as Margaret's survey of my new school clothes stopped at my feet. Her eyes were glued to my feet, and her jaw dropped. Her mouth froze agape, silent, as her eyes shot up to meet mine. She looked down again for a longer look at my freshly powdered white buck saddle shoes. This was different. These were not the standard brown and white leather school shoes we always wore.

I can't say I paid much attention to what she said at this point because I got so much satisfaction from the look in her eyes. I know how selfish that sounds. That emotion was not what I sought, but it was what I felt at that moment. I was standing at least a foot taller than normal, and the feeling was wonderful, overwhelming.

Finally I heard her, and the questions rapidly tumbled out.

"Where did you get those shoes? Why didn't you tell me? How much did they cost?"

I didn't even try to hide my excitement.

"I wanted to surprise you," I replied smugly.

I could tell she was annoyed, but I knew she would get over it quickly. Creating distance from this new element, we continued chattering about our skirts and blouses as we moved on our way to pick up Debbie. We knocked on the door. When it opened, a similar scene played out complete with wild shrieks and laughter from the three of us.

Her mom came to the door and told us to get on to school with all that noise. We hurried past two apartment buildings and came around a corner where Cookie and Evelyn waited for us. I didn't have to say a word. Amid the new and louder chorus of shrieks — the banter describing how we all looked as new sixth-graders — Debbie shouted out, "You gotta see Vicki's shoes. Those suckas are so cool, but you know white shoes are gonna get dirty real fast."

All eyes focused again on my feet. I did a little dance kick while Cookie and Evelyn stared at my feet, just as the others had done — confirmation that my shoes were a certified hit. This was the coolest I had ever felt. Inside I felt different, yes, special, and I loved it. Oh, the chatter continued all the way to school about classes we would take, which ones we would share, the teachers we would have, and, of course, where the boys would be.

The schoolyard met our expectations. We milled around with other friends, admired their clothes, commented on hair, and caught up on summer events. I felt that I was becoming a bit calculating, and I still had one more punch I wanted to deliver.

When the teacher released us for recess, I knew I had to pick just the right moment for my final display. I stored pent-up excitement over my hidden accessory.

I had held this secret from the Gibbs Girls ever since I returned from the Oakland department store. I waited for just the right moment when we were all playing on the playground, then I unveiled my secret weapon. Nonchalant, I truly acted like it was part of my routine. I stopped, reached into my purse, and took out a small white powder puff that came with the shoes.

Deliberately, yet casually, I began tapping both shoes from toe to sides erasing the small brown and green smudges that had dared to blemish them while I walked to school, bumped into stairs, or scraped chairs.

Jaws dropped. I will never forget the looks of awe among my friends on the playground that morning at Longfellow Elementary School. I was in another world. I have replayed that morning as I have embarked on new journeys or when spontaneously implementing something new. I may not know the reason, but I know that sixth-grade sense of enjoyment delivered a new-found boost in confidence I have never lost. I still savor the satisfaction of that day, the first time I was a standout in the crowd because of my new white bucks.

Anthony**Marcolongo**

A nthony Marcolongo, "Tony" to his friends, is a member of Northern California Publishers & Authors and lives in Lincoln, California.

He hails from New York and New England, which explains his proximity to Radcliffe College, former-ly an all-girl university in Cambridge, Massachusetts, with close ties to Harvard.

Known for his hat and sense of humor, Tony is a prolific writer and contributor to Sacramento-area critique groups. Notably, he is the author of the award-winning poem "The Sisters Of Pearl Harbor" regarding the World War II battleships Missouri and Arizona at the USS Arizona Memorial in Pearl Harbor, Hawaii.

The Halls of Radcliffe College

One night the older guys decided they were going to execute a panty raid at Radcliffe College. I had no idea what a "panty raid" was, nor what "Radcliffe College" was, because I was only 11 years old at the time, but I was up for the fun I expected.

Carmine produced a brochure of some kind, and all the guys went nuts.

I muscled my way to the table for a look. "The place looks like a library," I said.

Then they sat me in the booth of the coffee shop and explained that this "Radcliffe" was a school strictly for girls, and a panty raid was an illegal foray onto the college grounds in an attempt to obtain panties from the girls.

"They give them to you?" I asked.

Amid the roaring laughter that followed, Eddie told me that sometimes the girls did, and other times they had to be talked into it, but at no time were we allowed to harm or unduly embarrass any of the girls.

"So," he told me, "it comes down to a matter of ... salesmanship."

When everyone roared at that one, I did too, although I had no idea why.

As soon as it got dark, Charlie and Eddie showed up in their cars and Louie brought his station wagon with a wobbly old extension ladder sticking out the back.

Charlie told me to stay with the cars until the raid was over.

I said, "Sure thing. You bet, Charlie," but I had no such intention whatsoever. I was going on this raid, too.

When we parked, they quickly unlocked a gate and ran across the lawns, carrying the ladder and laughing all the way. I watched until they were out of sight, and then I ran in their direction.

When I cleared the brush, I saw the ladder leaning against the old red-colored stone walls of the dorm, resting against the sill of an open window. The guys were all off somewhere in the shadows of the campus.

I heard talking and giggling from the window above me. I may have been young, naive, and even a bit lame, but I was no coward. So, I steeled myself and scurried up the wobbly ladder.

When I reached the window, pandemonium broke out. There were at least four girls in the room in various stages of undress. At first they shrieked in unison, but then one of them said, "Oh my God! He's so cute!"

"What are you doing here?" they asked.

"I'm on a panty raid with my friends," I naively announced.

That's when they pulled me inside, and invited every girl on the floor to their room to see the youngster who had come to raid their panties. The room swelled with girls and each of them, one and two at a time, put on lipstick and kissed me all over my face and neck, giggling and smiling all the time. I loved it!

Next, each retrieved a pair of panties and stuffed them into my pockets and down my shirt.

What's your name, honey?" one of them asked.

The room fell silent as I announced, "I'm Tony."

"Ooh, how cute, can we keep him?" one of them swooned.

"Tony, you better go now, before the guards get back," instructed another.

And with that, they helped me back onto the ladder, at which point I could hear the guys running and shouting in the near darkness.

"Hurry Tony," the girls instructed, "and remember, we love you."

"We love you!" came a collective screaming laugh as I descended the ladder and dashed back to the car.

The guys arrived in a rush, jumped into the cars, and we sped off into the night, everyone roaring in delight.

We had traveled three or four blocks when Jimmy said, "Hey! Get a load of Tony's face, guys!"

Charlie tilted the rear-view mirror. His eyes popped wide-open, and he screeched the car to a stop.

As the other cars pulled up behind us, Charlie dragged me into their headlight beams. "How the hell did all that happen?" he demanded.

As I explained the events, Davy said, "Aw, baloney, you expect us to believe that?"

"Hey, wait a minute," said Carmine. "Check this out." And with that, he began pulling all those panties out of my pockets while I added the ones from inside my shirt.

The resultant reactions from all my pals should be obvious and need no explanation here. Suffice it to say that thanks to a bit of inner grit and the cooperation of that wobbly ladder, I became legendary almost overnight, in the coffee shop where we hung out, and in the halls of Radcliffe College.

Kiyo**Sato**

Kito Sato is the eldest child of a Japanese-American immigrant family. She and her family — eight brothers and sisters — were interned during World War II. She tells her heartfelt story in *Dandelion through the Crack,* which went on to win  the William Saroyan International Prize for Writing, the Sacramento County Historical Society Publications Award, the Northern California Publishers & Authors Gold Award, as well as the Best First Book Award.

Following her internment and, later, the end of the war, Kiyo joined the United States Air Force. She completed her education in nursing and achieved the rank of captain. Returning from military service, she married and started her own family in Sacramento.

During her career as a public health nurse, Kiyo developed the Blackbird Vision Screening System for detecting eye problems in children.

Kodomo-No-Tameni,
For the Sake of the Children

In this vast universe, two tiny, invisible cells come together attracted to each other. They grow into a blob. And then extensions appear with five toes and five fingers. Two eyeballs form. For nine months it grows with incredible precision, perfectly orchestrated.

The Conductor signals, and my journey starts. With the force of powerful tsunami waves, I am propelled down the birth canal. I reach the opening and look out. It is a "white" world out there. I am the wrong color. I am at the wrong place at the wrong time! I want to turn around and go back into my safe, warm place, but I have no choice.

The Conductor drops his baton; I am expelled!

It is the eighth day of May in 1923.

1926

I leave my baby brother sleeping in his strawberry crate in the shade of the Model-T farm truck and wander off to the next field where flowers are blooming around a puddle after the recent rain. Tiny yellow dandelions and pink lady slippers cover the ground like a carpet. I pick them one by one, carefully holding them in a tiny bouquet.

Jumping over ditches and walking down the long row, I reach Mama where she is picking strawberries. I give her the bouquet.

"How beautiful they are!" she says accepting them with both hands. She sits down on the ground and pushes her wide-brimmed straw hat back. She places the flowers carefully on the basket of strawberries.

"*Oyatsu?*" A snack? she asks.

She removes her hat and places it on the crate to protect the berries from the hot sun. She picks up the tiny flowers, takes my hand, and we walk to the end of the row where the old truck is parked. It is just in time as Seiji is attempting to climb out of his crate.

Mama gives me a graham cracker, unwraps the rice sacking kitchen towel and hands me a small Mason jar of warm cocoa. Unbuttoning her work shirt, she leans against the fender and feeds Seiji.

1933

We live on a 20-acre farm. Mama is constantly busy. She works in the strawberry field all day. She is round again. A brother or a sister is growing inside. I already have four brothers and a sister.

After supper, story time ends with pleas of "one more!"

"American stories are not good for children," Mama had said when I started school. Now, my father tells wonderful stories every night: Hiawatha, Japanese legends, Abraham Lincoln, *Les Miserables*, and the continuing saga of Kuzu, the not-so-smart boy we "adopt."

"*Ofuro* time!"

The children dash off to get their pajamas. In the bathhouse they shed their clothes and pile them by the old wringer washing machine where Mama will wash them.

Walking down the path each night with the youngest on his shoulder, my father looks up at the sky.

"Who can find the *Mitsu-boshi?*" It's the three stars in a row. *Mitsu* means three and *boshi* means stars. There they are every night, three stars in a row.

1937

My father comes home with an old Studebaker.

"Kiyo," he says, "You need to learn to drive." Ninth grade at Kit Carson Junior High School is ten miles into town, and we have no public transportation to get there.

I've driven the old Model-T on the farm since I was ten-years old, but this Studebaker is so different with gears to shift.

I drive the ten miles the next four years with a load of neighborhood kids, and then go on to enroll at Sacramento Junior College. For my parents, the American Dream is finally within reach.

JAPAN BOMBS PEARL HARBOR!

Seiji volunteers for the U.S. Army. I see my mother cry for the first time. She wants him to finish high school. My father thinks this may be the best thing for now. I think he is wishing that he had such an option.

"Once a Jap, always a Jap!" rings throughout the country. With a vengeance, General John L. DeWitt takes on the awesome task of corralling 120,000 of us, including orphans, with one-sixteenth or more "Japanese blood" into ten concentration camps.

Huge posters declare, "TO ALL THOSE OF JAPANESE ANCESTRY." They are nailed along our roads and buildings. I don't want to stop my Studebaker and read them.

"In ten days," it says, we are to leave with only what we can carry. The farm…the crop at its peak…our survival for the year…our dogs… our piano…. There is no time but to find old suitcases and pack my seven younger brothers and sisters for "the trip" while my parents work.

Late at night when the children are asleep, we discuss what has to be done.

"*Kodomo-no-tameni*," they say. Children must grow up happy and secure, Mama reminds us, as my parents face the monumental task of deciding what to do with our twenty acres and the house and all that we depended upon for survival.

1942

"Who can find the *Mitsu-boshi*?" my father says as we look up at the sky in the Arizona desert concentration camp, our ten cots lined up outside our barracks in the 127-degree heat.

"I see it!"

"They're over there!"

Clearer than we see them at home, there they are, the three stars in a row!

Never have we seen the stars so close. It is as if we are right in the middle of a galaxy!

1944

My brother Sanji, who was released to join me in Michigan to attend high school, gives me bus fare to go "home" from college.

The full moon shines upon the 50-acre sugar beet farm in Keenesburg, Colorado, with a small cabin and a windmill at its edge. My baby brother takes me by the hand to show me his bunk bed made from a locust tree his father had cut down with the tools he had smuggled into camp.

"Come outside. I want to show you our *ofuro* bath." Under the windmill neatly enclosed by four walls and a roof, there it is, a place to shed the day's soiled clothes and wash each other, and then to hop into the redwood tub, and soak, and make washcloth bubbles.

Above it the moon and the *Mitsu-boshi* shine.

1959

My children did not come through me. They were expelled, and I was not there. I cry not having been there to scoop my child in my hands, hold him in my arms, place him on my tummy and let him know that all is well.

1961

You come with tear-stained cheeks. You had rebelled when the social worker had to bodily get you in her car. You stand behind her seat all the way, crying. This is your third move, each time farther away from what had been "home" for almost four years.

I take you to your room. Carefully you place your one little, white sack of your belongings under the bunk bed after removing one toy, and walk back to the linoleum floor to play with your car alone.

We see you on Thursday and you were ours on Saturday. Why, I wonder, do we go clear across the ocean to adopt a child when in our own country hundreds of children are begging to belong to a family?

1963

Your head bobs from fatigue sitting upright in the back seat of our Volkswagen bus as we drive home from a day at the Lodi Grape Festival. Your sister and her father chat in front. I want to hold you, but you have not allowed anyone to touch you since you came. At almost three, the only person who can understand you is your sister who is ten months older than you. You two have a language all your own.

Many nights, I sit by your bed helplessly as you lash out with your nightmares. When you quiet down from exhaustion, I cover you up and let you sleep.

What is it that has been so frightening in your young life? What has happened that left you numb and unable to cry?

2003

"Thank you for loving me," a message says. No child should have to thank a parent for being loved. No child should have to be adopted. No child should be born and then shuttled off to foster care.

Where did the time go? My children are launched, my four precious Dandelions. My father's haiku describes it well:

> *Crushed by passing feet*
> *Growing through the pavement crack*
> *Dandelion Blooms*

I am now a dandelion *puff.* There is a *satori* that comes with age, a growth that comes through children, like a glimpse of a tiny diamond that appears in a coal that has been under pressure.

Soon a breeze will blow and gently send the seeds of the dandelion puff to places unknown. Life and death are seamless.

"*Kodomo-no-tameni.*"

My parents' legacy continues. The fifth generation thrives in multiethnic colors. Children know that they are priority. They are happy and secure. They go on to serve humanity. It is so simple.

A country is only as great as its caring for its children. Only then will we not have our children killing our children.

And the *Mitsu-boshi* shines on.

Denise Lee **Branco**

D enise Lee Branco spent her childhood on a California ranch, befriending furry and feathered residents, reading horse books, and competing in western horse shows. Compelled to write about a soul-to-soul connection and a bond she shared

with a horse for more than three decades, Denise began her literary career in 2008 after the passing of her beloved horse Freedom.

As a result, her first book, *Horse at the Corner Post: Our Divine Journey,* was introduced to the world in 2010. It not only won a silver medal in the 2011 Living Now Book Awards, but also has touched lives and assisted various charities in raising much-needed funds ever since.

Denise is a member of American Horse Publications, Women's Horse Industry Network, and Northern California Publishers & Authors. Visit her at www.HorseAtTheCornerPost.com.

Princess of Purpose

Around the globe mourners unite to bid farewell to a princess loved by so many — a princess who left a legacy destined to endure for generations. She gave unselfishly and opened her heart to others time and time again. Her kindness and compassion toward others proved endless — evidence that she remained grounded despite her royalty. She was the one and only Diana, the Princess of Wales. They say, when one life leaves this earth plain, another arrives.

* * *

Across the Pond, a ball of red fur lay curled on a matted bed of green clover. The newborn bovine had not moved from her cozy bed overnight. It was birthing season on a California cattle ranch and time for the rancher's wife, Jean, to make her daily herd check.

The daily count revealed a plus-one mismatch. The count could mean only one thing: the unassuming red calf was a twin, abandoned by its mother. Often, a cow will abandon one twin when she instinctively feels she cannot provide adequate nourishment for two calves. Sadly, the orphaned calf must fend for itself. It will sneak up behind other cows when their own calf is drinking milk and then try to join in for dinner. Typically the cow will kick or head-butt the orphaned calf away within seconds.

Jean knew from experience this was a lose-lose situation; the newborn needed tender loving care. She retraced her steps to the hay barn and fetched a wheelbarrow, so she could rescue this inno-cent soul destined for greatness. As Jean lifted the abandoned twin into the wheelbarrow, the famished calf welcomed the help of her guardian angel. Content and curled up in the center of the wheel-barrow, the newborn glowed with a sense of peace. She relaxed, despite the rather bumpy ride to her new home in the barn.

A nameless addition to a family of humans and pets, the newborn needed a name. In honor of Princess Diana who blessed the world – and who had passed that same week – this newborn gift from God was named Princess.

While Princess waited patiently, the rancher's wife prepared the first of many bottle feedings — a plastic bottle full of powdered, nutrient-rich milk and warm water. The calf practically inhaled the mixture as if it were a new invention in short supply. From that point on, Princess was hooked! Whenever she saw the rancher's wife approaching during feeding time, sucking sounds and bellow-ing ensued. Though she could not speak, the little heifer made it obvious she craved another bottle of powdered milk.

Princess thrived and tackled life head on. This young bovine seemed uninfluenced by differences and enjoyed making friends with humans, dogs, cats, and the many creatures that call a ranch home. The calf's tranquil demeanor gave an impression that her inner Labrador retriever was fighting to come out. Princess and the German shepherd hit it off instantly. She bucked and head-butted him while he pogoed up and down, playfully grabbing onto her mouth with his razor-sharp teeth. The two became inseparable playmates.

Once while Princess and the German shepherd were playing un-fettered in the yard, Princess spotted the rancher's wife at the front door of the house. It was about that time of day — dinner —and Princess knew it. The rancher's wife slipped indoors to mix her formula for the red calf. Bottle in hand, Jean turned the corner of the hallway on her way back to the front door. Surprise! Princess stepped into the house. Once her slippery hooves set foot on the waxed linoleum flooring, she became Bambi on slick ice!

Princess followed the rancher's wife around like a dog, so Jean tried fastening a dog collar around the calf's neck. She took her on walks outside the confines of the backyard. As Princess grew with each passing day, the dog-imposter walks turned into people walks; Princess took off running with the rancher's wife flailing behind.

Princess did not limit her friendships to bovines; she was friendly to all creatures. When a grief-stricken horse named Freedom lost his longtime horse buddy to a terminal illness, Princess was summoned to comfort Freedom and ease his loneliness. The ranchers placed gelding and heifer in adjoining corrals during Freedom's bereavement. They bonded. They chose the same area of the fence to rest near. Simultaneously they would lean against the boards and stretch through for a fleeting nose-touch. The friendship blossomed.

When the day came for Princess to be bottle-weaned, Jean felt it was time to return the heifer to the cattle herd, but her thoughts quickly changed when barnyard behaviors swayed her conventional wisdom.

Jean led Princess out of the adjoining corral towards the pasture gate, but she heard whinnying from behind. Distracted, she slowed the calf's pace and glanced over her left shoulder. Freedom whinnied and paced frantically. The farther the human-bovine duo walked, the more hysterical the equine became. It was obvious. The unspoken language between gelding and heifer proved that they were meant to be together. Jean felt there was no option. Freedom still needed Princess. So Jean moved the pair to a corner paddock near the cattle herd where they could be together for months to come.

And when it was time for Princess to move on and bear "children" of her own, she did not forget her tall, equine friend. Even with a calf in tow, Princess lounged near the fence line of Freedom's paddock, stretching for an occasional nose-touch with her friend.

Just as the Princess of Wales befriended and cared for others without prejudice, the little red heifer, the namesake Princess, instinctively knew her purpose: to support in time of need, making a difference in the lives of God's creatures.

Dennis **Potter**

Dennis Potter is the creator of the character Jake Burns. Dennis and his family live in Lincoln, California where he is developing the Jake Burns series.

In his upcoming book chronicles, Dennis takes  Jake Burns into a tunnel system where he discovers the clothed skeleton of Colonel Hara Yoshida. Jake's determination to see the return of Colonel Yoshida to his family is a test of his character and becomes a watershed change in his life. Jake Burns is the uncommon, common man. Through all his lives, Jake attacks life with enthusiasm, determination, and humor, equally at home eating a hot dog from a street vendor or attending a ballet. In his short story, "Best Friend," Dennis exposes Jake as an eleven-year-old prodigy.

Communicate with Dennis at DennisPotter56@ aol.com.

Best Friend

I am mad at my new neighbors. I haven't met them yet, but I'm mad at them.

My very best friend ever moved out of the state, off the planet. Gary and I had lived next door to each other since we were born. We became best friends in kindergarten. The summer was going to be great, and our plans for the sixth grade would have made us kings. Now his house is empty. So am I. So is my summer. I don't care who is moving next door. I want my best friend back.

I sat on the front porch depressed and angry. Usually I solve problems, but this was different. Not even the antics of squirrels could cheer me. Two cars pulled into Gary's driveway. The driver of the first was Mr. Winkel, the Realtor; I wasn't happy with him either. My mother stepped onto the porch with a glass of milk and chocolate chip cookies – an obvious tonic for my funk. I would eat the cookies: but they wouldn't change my disposition. The driver of the second car stepped out, and I faced surprise. He was a tall Asian; I thought all Asians were short. Then he waved at our porch. My mom waved back. As the two men entered Gary's house, I asked my mom, "Who was that?"

"That's Mr. Honda. He and his family are moving in next door.

You were at Grandpa's farm when he came over to introduce himself; he seems like a nice man."

"He's tall."

"Yes, a little taller than your Uncle Jack. He has three children. I think he said two boys and one girl. I forget what their ages are. Now, Jake, I expect you to be nice to that family. I know you miss Gary, but the Hondas had nothing to do with his family moving. OK?'

"Yes ma'am."

"I mean it. Now finish the milk and cookies, and get to work weeding the front flower bed."

I took my frustrations out on the weeds, pulling them out of their comfortable existence. I mumbled to myself, "This is my mother's flower bed. Why do I have to weed the darn thing?" Just then a small garter snake darted out from some weeds. I jumped back and landed on my butt. A squirrel on a tree limb laughed at me, so I was startled again when the shadow of a man fell over me. Looking up, I saw Mr. Honda.

"Are you OK?"

I stood up. "Yes, sir. A snake startled me. I don't like snakes."

"Neither do I. You must be Jake. I'm Thomas Honda."

"Thomas?" I asked, exposing my bewilderment.

"I was born and raised here in California," he said. "The only person in our family born in Japan is my daughter Maiko."

Mr. Honda studied me. "I need some help," he said. "I've been told by many people around here that you solve problems and give good advice."

"Sometimes, sir."

"My children have lived most of their lives in Japan. They are not thrilled with the idea of moving here. What do you think I could do to help ease their transition here?"

I pondered the problem as we moved to sit on the front porch steps. "They are losing friends and being placed into a strange culture," I said. "I would let them fix up their rooms as they like. Their bedrooms will become familiar – just what they were used to, comfortable. Once in a while, you could serve them food that they liked in Japan. Make one room truly Japanese. You and your wife must also be leaving many good friends behind."

"To give them, us, something that is comfortable," Mr. Honda repeated.

"Yes, sir." I looked out at the grass. "I think my friend Gary must be going through the same thing."

"Your father told me about your friend. Moving is always difficult. I have to go now; thank you for your advice."

"You're welcome, sir, but, you knew what to do before you came over here."

Mr. Honda stood up and looked at me. "Jake, if you want a job in the future, come see me."

Mr. Honda got into his car and drove off. My mother came beside me. "Are you finished with the weeding?" she asked.

"No, I was talking to Mr. Honda." I looked down at my feet. "Mom, I like Mr. Honda."

"That's nice, Jake, but what's wrong?"

Tears formed in my eyes. "I feel like a traitor to Gary."

Mom sat down and pulled me to her side. "You're not a traitor," she said. "Gary will always be your friend. You both will have new people and things to experience. When you talk on the phone, you two will be able to share these new experiences, and it will draw you closer."

Mom kissed the top of my head. "You can finish the weeding tomorrow," she said. "Why don't you ride your bike to the park and think things over? Just be back here by dinner time."

Over the next couple weeks, the Honda house hosted a frenzy of activity. Contractors started extensive remodeling. Mr. Honda invited me in to show the changes. He turned one section of the house into a small piece of Japan. Isolated from the rest of the house, the room required us to remove our shoes and wear slippers. I was struck by the space's simplicity and the tranquility of its lighting. It wasn't ornate, but it spoke of elegance; it showed class.

Mr. Honda asked me, "I have a job for you. Think you can do it?"

"What do you want?"

"A couple things. When the movers bring in the rest of our furniture, I can't be available. Mr. Winkel will be supervising the move. I would like you to make sure that no one enters the Japanese room. Can you do that?"

"Yes, sir."

"Good. The second thing is, when the movers are done, I would like you to take pictures of my children's bedrooms and e-mail them to my wife."

"So your kids can see what they look like and maybe make changes," I said. Sensing something was not right I added. "Sir, I would like to modify that. I will only go into the bedrooms if your designers are with me."

"Ok, but why?"

"If I went in alone, it would be like I snuck into their rooms. That would compromise the...the..."

"Sanctity of their rooms," he said.

"Yes, sir, the sanctity of the rooms; thank you."

Mr. Honda put his hands on his hips. "How do you plan to keep those big mover men out of the main room?"

"Put up a *shoji* screen," I said.

Mr. Honda laughed then asked, "How do you know about *shoji* screens?"

"I'm doing my homework." I said, looking up into Mr. Honda's eyes. "I know there are other reasons why you are doing this."

"What would that be?"

"You are helping me get through losing my best friend. You are getting me involved with your family to help them get through this move and the loss of their best friends."

My new neighbor swerved his head. "That's it!" he said, waving his hand. "Buy a suit; you go on my staff today!"

Finally, the entire Honda family started moving into their house. Realtors and interior designers lined up at the front porch like expectant parents.

I stayed home while my parents traveled to my grandpa's farm. They wanted to convince him to move into the city near us. I told them that wouldn't work, but they didn't listen. But, because I told them what they didn't want to hear, they gave me extra chores to do

Extracting weeds from the front lawn, I heard the squirrels discussing my work again. I ignored them and removed another dandelion when a large black SUV swept into the Honda driveway. I stopped to watch the action.

Mr. Winkel advanced to the SUV and greeted Mr. Honda as he stepped out. Mr. Honda looked tense. I knew he wanted his family to be happy.

More doors opened, and I finally saw the rest of the Honda family. Mrs. Honda was trim. As I expected, she dressed well. The two sons came into view. They were older than me, in their mid-teens. It was clear they soon would be as tall as their father. Last out was the daughter. She was my age, carrying herself erect, and the sun shimmered off her beautiful black hair. I watched the groups introduce themselves, entering into a bowing contest, but the squirrels nagged me to get back to work. I returned to the weeds.

Another dandelion met its fate while I ran a couple jazz tunes through my head.

"Jake."

I looked up to see Mr. and Mrs. Honda. I stood up and quickly brushed off my jeans.

"Janice, this is Jake, the young man who helped me with the house. What's this, Jake? More weeds to remove?"

"Yes, sir. I got in a little trouble with my folks, so I get to remove more weeds."

Eyes opened when I switched to Japanese and said, "Mrs. Honda, it is very nice to meet you." She answered me in a barrage of Japanese.

I returned to English, saying, "Mrs. Honda, I have worked for two weeks to greet you in Japanese. I outsmarted myself, and that one sentence is all I know."

Mrs. Honda smiled and reverted to English: "That was considerate of you. I understand that you put together the montages in our children's rooms."

"Yes ma'am," I said. "I thought it would help them see a connection between Japan and America."

Mr. Honda said, "The baseball montages for my sons with photos of Japanese players and U.S. players, stadiums, and fans were a huge hit with them. But Jake, how did you find the same thing with the ballet dancers?"

"I went to a ton of web sites and begged for anything I could get I visited a couple dance studios to get some information. Now I get hundreds of e-mails. They think I'm a fanatic."

Mr. Honda interrupted, "See, dear, this is why he is going to sit at my side in the boardroom. At age eleven, he can get more done than most of my staff."

The squirrels started chattering. "What is wrong with the squirrels?" Mr. Honda asked.

"I haven't given them their daily ration of nuts," I said. "My family loves to watch this. You might, too."

I walked to my porch, retrieved a small paper bag and settled at the center of the lawn. Opening the bag, I placed the nuts on the ground in front of me. The squirrels read the signal. They scampered out of the tree and climbed over me to get the nuts. All but two grabbed and ran; they sat in front of me eating. I looked at Mr. and Mrs. Honda, "This is Hank and Mabel."

Mrs. Honda said, "We would like you to meet the rest of our family now."

Mabel climbed onto my lap, and Hank onto my shoulder. "Thank you, Mrs. Honda," I said, resignation in my voice. "But...but they need time today to settle in. I have to finish here or else I'll get more chores to do. It took my friend Gary some time before he was ready to explore outside his new home. For your kids this is going to be harder than it was for him. Everything is different. When they are ready, I'll be here.

"And, oh, Mr. Honda, some small gifts are on the porch, from my family to your family. Would you mind getting them; I'm kind of stuck here."

Mrs. Honda smiled at me, "I can see that Hank and Mabel have you pinned to that spot."

Mr. Honda retrieved the packages, and the Hondas went back to their new house. Hank and Mabel finally went back to their tree, and I went back to the weeds.

Two days later I was in the office of Mr. Hanson, the owner of a small manufacturing company, and we discussed whether he should upgrade some of his equipment. The crux of the discussion was that his existing machine could produce the needed parts, but it was slow. A newer machine would be faster and control quality better, but it would not be cheap. Mr. Hanson and I considered work that a new machine could possibly bring when my cell phone sounded off.

"Hi dad, what's up?"

"Jake, we have some guests; get yourself back home."

"I need about five more minutes with Mr. Hanson."

"Make it a fast two minutes and peddle fast."

"Yes, sir. Bye, dad."

"You have to leave?" asked Mr. Hanson.

"Yes sir."

"So…"

"Get the new machine," I advised. "The old one is breaking down almost daily."

"I will think it over, Jake; now get home, I can't afford to have you grounded again."

I raced home at top speed; I didn't cut across our lawn. The last time I cut across the lawn on my bicycle I found myself grounded for a week. I entered the house and found my parents in our living room along with the Honda family.

"Jake, you made good time," said my dad.

"Yes, sir."

"Did you and Mr. Hanson reach a decision?"

"I think so," I said. "He will get the new machine and scrap the old one. Mr. and Mrs. Honda, it is nice to see you."

"It is our pleasure to see you again, said Mr. Honda.. "What does this Mr. Hanson pay you?"

"I get all of his scrap metal from his processes," I answered.

"That doesn't sound like a good bargain," said Mrs. Honda.

"Oh, yes it is. I hire a trucking company to take it to a recycling center. After I pay the hauler, I clear about one hundred dollars a week after taxes. Mr. Hanson's business couldn't pay me that much."

Mr. Honda studied me: "One hundred dollars a week? And you never touch the scrap?"

My dad added, "He has four other scams that do about the same. Jake gets to keep twenty-five percent, and the rest goes into a college fund."

Mr. Honda changed the subject, saying, "Jake, I would like to introduce you to my offspring." In a stage whisper, he added, "If I call them *my children,* they get mad at me." He returned to a normal voice: "The young man on the far side is James, next to him is Samuel, and last, but not least my daughter Maiko."

Before I can react, my dad exclaimed, "Son, you put your mother and me in a bad light."

"What did I do wrong?"

"It's not what you did wrong; it is what you did right."

Dad turned to the new neighbors: "Mr. and Mrs. Honda, the gifts you received from this family, in truth, only came from Jake. He picked them out; he paid for them."

Mrs. Honda asked, "You picked out that lovely vase?"

"With a lot of help. Does it fit the room?" I asked.

"It looks as if it were made for that room," she said.

I filled in the details: "Mr. Stevens and I looked at photos of your 'Japanese room' for several hours before we settled on what to make."

My mother asked, "You bought the vase from Mr. Stevens?"

"Yes, I got a good deal."

"Jake, where did the money come from? Mom asked, "Not your school fund, I hope!"

"Mom, we shouldn't discuss that now."

"Jake."

"It came from my car fund," I said.

"What car fund?"

"Of the twenty-five percent I get from my operations, I put half of that into a car fund," I explained. "The other half is split in half again. One part goes to fun stuff; the other part goes into a slush fund. I didn't want to dip that deep into my slush fund, so I borrowed from the car fund."

Mrs. Honda asked, "Who is this Mr. Stevens?"

"Mr. Stevens is a local artist," Mom answered. "His glass vases are in high demand."

Mrs. Honda surmised: "High demand translates into a high price." She turned her head to me. "Jake, you shouldn't have done that; it is too much."

"No ma'am it isn't too much," I said. "I saw how much you were doing to make your family comfortable in your move. I thought you and Mr. Honda might need a little something too."

Mr. Honda emphatically stated: "You will work for me young man, thank you. Now you have what? Five years before you can drive?"

"No, sir. Three years."

My parents grinned, and the Hondas sat stunned. Mrs. Honda asked, "But you are only eleven, and the driving age is 16, right?"

"In one month I will be 12," I explained. "There is a rule in the licensing code that says if you are involved in farm work you can get your license at 15. I do enough work on my Grandfather's and my Uncle Jack's farms that I qualify."

Maiko spoke to me for the first time: "What type of car are you going to buy?"

"I'm on the lookout for an old pickup truck," I said. "Get the engine, brakes, and other stuff up to new. With your parents' permission, we could go for some rides together."

Maiko's eyes sparkled. Just like that, I realized that I had found my new best friend. Maiko said, "Thank you for the montage in my bedroom. I love it."

"You're very welcome, Maiko," I answered.

"Jake, could I watch you feed the squirrels?" she asked.

"Better than that," I said. "You can help me feed them."

"When?"

"Why not now?"

"Father, may I?" Maiko begged.

Mr. Honda smiled and nodded yes. I took Maiko's hand, and we went outside. Mom picked up on the gesture and said to my father, "Don, we might have to allow Jake to increase his take to thirty percent."

Mr. Honda quickly added a comment: "Mrs. Burns, you are right. Jake's slush fund is about to suffer."

Terry **Burke Maxwell**

Terry Burke Maxwell, now in Sacramento, re-flects on her San Franciscan roots with "Values and Valuables," a story of grandparents she never knew. After a teaching career, Terry moved to a

publishing position in elementary mathematics: writing teacher manuals, editing textbooks, and producing resource supplements.

Next Terry became a tech writer and trainer in the computer industry. Still committed to education, she has reprinted some of her materials for basic math and computers: *The CompuResource Book* for activities, *Arithmetic In English* for vocabulary, and *Fractions* and *Decimals* for basic math skills. Recently, Terry has published a memoir, *Eye from the Edge*, by Californian Ruben Llamas, under the Maxwell Group's imprint Earth Patch Press. All are listed in *Books In Print*.

Visit www.tmgpubco.com or www.earthpatch-press.com.

Values and Valuables

"Adolf! Adolf! Do you have Gladys with you?" Theresa shouted over the rumbling roar as the house shook and the floors undulated beneath her. Shadows from the early dawn's sunlight jumped along the moving walls. Theresa grabbed her robe and the bedpost in one lunge, heading toward the hall.

"I have her! She is fine!" Already in the small nursery room beside their bedroom, Adolf lifted his newest, twenty-month-old daughter, the fourth — his afterthought as he called her later — and started down the hall. The floor was like a ribbon blowing in waves that threw them side-to-side. An enormous roar vibrated through Adolf's ears to his legs as he stumbled to the stairs.

"Carin, Ebba, Anna! Are you coming? Throw on anything. Meet us downstairs, outside."

The morning was Wednesday, April 18, 1906. The time was 5:13 a.m. Like some other San Francisco homes, this tall sturdy house shook but did not break; it was twisted but did not bend. It became disheveled, but would remain whole and standing. The house creaked, groaned and wobbled. The first strong rotational thrust had thrown everyone around. Beds turned ninety degrees. People landed on the floor. For many, doors were stuck or blocked by large armoires and heavy bureaus. Bricks from chimneys fell through windows or out onto the street. Many awoke from a sound sleep. Those who could ran for the outside.

After arcing like a ball along the track of a roulette wheel, the floors now seemed to ripple beneath their feet. Adolf kept bumping into the wall as he stepped carefully downstairs, holding Gladys tight to his chest. Remarkably she was not squirming or crying. As Adolf reached the bottom of the stairs, Ebba offered her arms to take her youngest sister. "Papa, let me have her."

Relieved, Adolf grabbed his coat from the pile of clothes near the fallen clothes rack. He thrust his shoulder forward to open the front door and ran to the street. The roaring groans from the earth's spectacular performance had stopped. Adolf's feet gripped familiar solid dirt. Clatter from falling debris faded. For a minute or two an amazing silence came over everything, and everyone.

Neighbors stood still, staring at each other, their street, their homes, until a sudden crash of a stairway, or the shattering of window glass, startled them again. They just looked around, not realizing yet how lucky they were. Yes, most of the Victorian houses on this length of Folsom Street were still standing. But evidence of this earthquake's magnitude was very visible: the broken staircases, the glass shards covering sidewalks and front gardens. A few houses leaned into the street like drunken sailors against a pole.

As if everyone took a big breath together, parents hugged their children and each other. Still in Ebba's arms, Gladys broke the silence with a strong cry, shocking her sisters out of their immobile stances. It was morning and time for a change and food. Theresa took Gladys, giving her a hug and kisses, and passed her back to Ebba.

Adolf and Theresa spoke to their neighbors, discovering that everyone close by seemed to have come through this enormous earthquake without immediate serious loss. Theresa motioned to twelve-year old Carin. Together mother and daughter walked to the other side of the street, stepping over cracks in the surface and rubble from fallen window boxes and broken wagons with useless wheels. Further down they saw Mrs. Keller's house and stable, both still standing with only a few fallen fence posts around the side and back.

Theresa and Carin greeted their neighbor Emma. Always an early riser, Emma told how the unusual neighing of the horses woke her up minutes before the quake. But the six or seven horses the folks kept in these stables were quiet now. Theresa walked over to Abby, their brown mare, who snorted and pawed at the dirt, stepping around nervously. Theresa put her hands on the strong brown jaw, rubbing Abby's smooth nose. Theresa ran her hand along the mare's firm back and legs. The mare seemed fine, finally nuzzling her owner and snorting with relief. How long would it be before Theresa would hitch Abby to the wagon to take Adolf downtown to Shreve & Co where he was a master Silversmith? Would such simple and pleasant routines ever return?

But now, they needed to fill some buckets with water. Carin found two wooden buckets, made by her grandfather, Theresa's father Rudolph, the cooper. Carin held a bucket under the spout of the tall hand pump, while Theresa grabbed the iron handle with both of her hands. Would the well still give the fresh water they had relied on for almost twenty years? The water spurted and spouted, but then it poured out in streams with every downward pull. This was very good news. Mrs. Keller's well was working! It would continue to fill every bucket a person could find. And those buckets of water helped to put out a nearby fire before it turned into an inferno. For this day, their Mission Valley neighborhood was spared. This well, plus some water from springs on the nearby hill, would supply the neighborhood, their horses, even their new-fangled automobiles for many more years to come.

When Theresa and Carin returned to Adolf and the others, people were moving around but still in shock. News spread of other neighborhoods. The Braese family began to realize that other areas were much worse. Even so no one wanted to return to the house let alone sleep indoors. But they did need food and water. And the girls wanted to find other clothes. Adolf and Theresa gingerly entered their house. Things were all thrown about: vases, some furniture broken, and dishes all over the kitchen floor in pieces. But they had pots and pans to use. After finding more suitable clothes, they decided to learn of their nearby relatives. Theresa, who had founded the local Parents-Teachers Association, wanted to see the nearby school. They agreed to return in an hour.

Adolf ran to Market Street and was horrified to see the devastation. He ran as far down as he could, only to be stopped by piles of crumpled buildings, crates, and boxes, even a wagon with a dead horse, and streetcar tracks buckled in the middle of the road. Adolf struggled to walk through jumbled cobblestones, jumping over a large gap in the street. He joined a group of men and asked about downtown. He asked about the new Shreve & Company building. Its architectural strength and aesthetic interior beauty had been the recent talk of the town. Word was that the building and a few others like it had survived the earthquake! The architectural frame had held. Adolf breathed a sigh of relief. But he looked around and thought where will we get customers even if we have a building? He spotted a friend from Shreve's, "Henry, how is your family? Your home?"

Henry's reply was sobering. "Adolf, our house is useless. My wife took the children to a friend's house on Church Street. Everything around us is in shambles. We are talking about leaving and going to Los Angeles. I have a friend there who wants me to join him in his shop in Central Los Angeles. Come with me, Adolf. With your talent and my business skills we would have customers lining up at the door for your silver work. And you could work with that gold-in-quartz you keep talking about—those nuggets you brought with you from Colorado years ago."

Adolf was trying to take it all in. "Right now, Henry, I want to get back to Folsom Street. I will consider this idea. Talk to me again, especially if you work out definite plans. And let me know if Shreve's is going to open."

Adolf started back to Folsom Street. He smelled something. When he realized it was smoke, his heart lurched. The smell of smoke was blowing from the northwest side of Market Street. A few plumes of black smoke were rising above the destruction. Spaces that once were filled with a building provided a view of the growing smoke clouds. He started walking faster. People around him were too. Fire, San Francisco's demon, would scorch or destroy anything standing: homes, small stores and large buildings, boarding houses and hotels — even the grand Palace Hotel.

He ran the rest of the way to Folsom Street. Breathless, he let his daughters tell him the news about Theresa's many relatives. No bad injuries. And most of their houses in need of only minor repairs. Then they looked at Adolf. He simply pointed to the area of the smoke clouds getting bigger and bigger, now visible above the houses.

They knew that they could walk east to the Bay. They began to select warm coats, food staples, tents and quilts for sleeping. Theresa ran over to the Keller's stables. Horse owners decided that a few men would stay with the horses in the stables where they would be near the well, if the fire came this far. A few relatives and neighbors also decided to stay at their homes for now. Theresa, Adolf, their daughters, one of Theresa's brothers, all headed east to San Bruno Ave, wondering what was ahead of them. The streets were full of others with carts and people loaded with large baskets.

The next few days at their camp were frustrating for the Braese girls. They were glad to be away from the burning neighborhoods. But they felt so helpless. By playing with Gladys they kept themselves entertained between the chores of the day. So for this brief respite Gladys had lots of attention. At the end of the day they walked up the Potrero Hill to see the city burn. The smoke clouds were enormous. They could hear the explosions of dynamite thrown by the soldiers to create a firebreak. Then a short time later a new plume of smoke appeared where no fire had been. Clouds would diminish in one area but in another the sky became a flaming mix of orange, red, and purple.

Along Market Street the devastated buildings included San Francisco's newspapers industry. West of Market Street most of downtown was leveled. Help began to arrive. Oakland sent a fire engine over on a ferry. U.S. Navy ships sailed in through the Golden Gate and brought sailors who helped save what was left of Telegraph Hill, and near downtown, the many piers along the waterfront.

The inferno moved to homes south and west. But very wide Dolores Street became a firebreak. At the south side of Dolores Street near Howard and 18th, men took doors off houses to serve as a firewall. Each man held a door against the oncoming fire. In the intense heat, they heard and felt the paint blister but they held on and the fire went no further on that street. Meanwhile on 20th Street above Mission Park others stopped the fire, helped by water from the springs of the 21st street hill. Along with fresh water from wells like Mrs. Keller's, these local water sources saved more houses than were saved by dynamite in inexperienced hands. By Saturday morning the Mission area was declared safe.

By late Saturday the Braese family moved home. They now could sleep in their homes but not cook there. Chimneys had to be inspected before indoor cooking could begin again. So they set up a sidewalk stove and table. They added a slanted roof and sides—and glad they did when it rained a few days later.

Adolf learned that Shreve's new building had survived the earthquake but the fire had demolished the handsome interior. He thought Shreve's might never open again. He began to assess his tools and resources. The thought of moving to Los Angeles seemed more and more necessary.

"Adolf, what are you looking for?" Theresa found Adolf rummaging in his tool trunk. The trunk had followed him across the ocean from Stockholm, through his employment at Tiffany's in New York, and then by rail westward.

"Remember, Theresa, how I told you about the wily miner from Colorado that I knew? He was the one who had me work so hard. Then he picked my brain to learn what nuggets were the richest in gold. And poof, one morning he was gone, taking most of my findings, and the maps."

Theresa felt such relief to be home next to her warm fun loving, good husband. Then her eyes caught a sparkle of gold from a small black quartz nugget he was holding, one of his few remaining pieces.

"What are you thinking, Adolf?"

"Perhaps our future would be better elsewhere. I have lost my place here. The new Shreve's building withstood the earthquake, but the interior shiny wood, the mirrored walls and marble counters are ruined. What a job to rebuild, if they do. It will never be as beautiful, and it would take time. Besides I have always dreamt of having a Braese company here in America like my father's silver factory in Stockholm. To design jewelry and silver pieces of my choice — that would be very special. Henry — you have met him— is talking about moving to Los Angeles. He is very capable and a good businessman. We are planning to set up our own silversmith and jewelry shop in central Los Angeles."

Theresa stepped back, stunned at what her husband was saying. "Oh, Adolf, how can you even think of moving down there? We are among the early San Franciscans. We have so many relatives here. My life is here. I was born here. Our daughters would be horrified to have to move south. I cannot even imagine it. San Francisco will come back and be better than ever. It has to!"

"I may not have a choice, Theresa. My work place is gone. For if Shreve does come back, it will take many, many months, or years even. In the mean time I need to bring in money for our family. I have enough of my tools to continue. But I need a different place. Henry and I will be set up very quickly. I will begin my work as soon as I get there."

Adolf avoided telling her that he had already told Henry he would go. He must take this opportunity. He turned to look at the quartz nuggets sitting on the soft flannel cloth he wrapped them in. The milky white quartz was so similar to the black quartz. Thin gold striations feathered each nugget, but against contrasting color. He looked at Theresa and thought of how he would miss her in Los Angeles.

"I don't see any other solution. I need a place for my trade. And San Francisco might not recover as you hope." He put his arms around her and held her close, kissing her gently. "We will work this out. I must get back to work. Meanwhile, I want to get on a steamer in a couple of days. I have much to prepare."

Theresa tried to absorb this terrible news. But she knew he was right, and that she would manage. She had to. She would help her parent teacher groups rebuild the schools. She would still have her brothers and sisters, and her daughters, and her father. If only her mother were still alive — gone now for 6 years. Mathilda, the strong Swedish seamstress and milliner, had been their stronghold. Theresa fought the tears. She took a big breath and looked at Adolf.

"I know you are doing what you must, my dear husband. But I believe San Francisco will be rebuilt, better than before. I believe that you will return here, hopefully sooner than you think. But I am not going to think about that now. I must get out to our sidewalk stove and put together a meal. I have mouths to feed and neighbors to help and schools to rebuild, and a household to arrange. My brother George will help me and the girls are very capable. We will be fine."

With that Theresa picked up her long skirt and whisked out of the room before Adolf could catch his breath. "What am I doing," he thought. But his plan was in place. He had a few days before he would sail from the San Francisco port. He placed the gold nuggets into the black bag and put the bag in a small wooden box. He would make something from these, and many other things as well. Theresa would be proud of him when she joined him again, not just with money for living, but also with valuables that would last longer than either of their lives. He walked firmly downstairs with renewed purpose. Thank God their house was among the few spared by major damage from either the earthquake or the fire.

He was anxious to return to his art. The sooner he could begin, the sooner he and his family would be together, hopefully in Los Angeles.

> *"The further you are from the last big earthquake,*
> *the nearer you are to the next."*
>
> —Perry Byerly
> Department of Seismology,
> University of California

***

Bronson, William. *The Earth Shook, The Sky Burned* Doubleday & Company, Inc., Garden City, N.J., 1959. 192 pp.

Mack, Gristle. *1906 Surviving San Francisco's Great Earthquake and Fire.* Chronicle Books, S.F. CA 94102, 1981. 128 pp

Thomas, Gordon and Witts, Max Morgan. *The San Francisco Earthquake* Stein and Day Publishers, New York, N.Y. 10017, 1971. 316 pp

Hills of San Francisco (Foreword by Herb Caen). The Chronicle Publishing Company. "Compiled from a series of articles which appeared in The San Francisco Chronicle" Copyright, 1959. Distributed by Norse Publishing Company, San Carlos, California

The Armstrong and Braese Families. Book Two: The Family and Descendants of Heinrich Adolf Braese and Johanna Matilde Mueller. Compiled by Terry Burke Maxwell, 2001.

The Descendants of Thomas Burke and Sally Fahy of Cloonkeen, Athenry, Galway. Notes for Bernard, p 13. Compiled by Terry Burke Maxwell, 2002. (Reference: *Burke / Lawless Genealogy* Compiled by Terry Burke Maxwell 2003)

Ted**Witt**

Ted Witt started his professional writing career as a newspaper reporter along the Central Coast of California and then in San Diego County. He moved to Northern California to transition

into the profession of public relations. Eventually he migrated to executive management positions, including an eight-year stint as executive director of the California Association of School Business Officials. Currently he is the vice president of national initiatives at the Epylon Corporation, a consulting and management company serving schools.

As an avocation, Ted started the publishing company Pretty Road Press, specializing predominately in books on business and school administration. He is the author of *No One Ever Told Me That.*

He's known to pursue a new hobby at the start of every year. This year it is raising chickens.

Follow him on Twitter: @TedWitt1, and meet Dee Dee at www.MostFamousChicken.com.

World's Most Famous Chicken

No amount of planning prepares you for life's turns. Just around the corner a peculiar hobby, preposterous adventure, or a parade of poultry employs you. Serendipity tracks you down, like it or not. So never could I have imagined I would husband two hens, let alone become biographer of the world's most famous chicken.

Of course, by now you've heard of Dee Dee, seen her on Facebook, and repeated stories of her near-death experiences. After all, she is famous, gossip fodder, and paparazzi bait.

She arrived unexpectedly on my birthday.

"I'm too tired to go out to dinner," said my wife, returning from work, "so I stopped by KFC."

Nancy held out a red and white bucket of Kentucky Fried Chicken. She hates fast-food chicken, and she secretly suspects Colonel Sanders' heirs of fowl crimes. Nancy acted out of character patronizing the former Pepsi subsidiary. How odd!

Flustered, I said, "You didn't have to do anything," and I grabbed the bucket. Unusually light, the container housed noise. Inside, I found two live chicks, sisters of the Orpington clan. Suddenly, life turned and assigned me a new role as a suburban farmer.

The chicks needed names. The outgoing, clumsy one, yellow and slight, earned the name Flip, a gender-neutral handle with a hint of in-your-face feminism.

The other, Dee Dee, like the preponderance of American celebrities, inherited her name and fell into her fame by accident. A children's book proposal sat on my desk about Dee Dee, a run-away chicken. I had been pondering book titles — *Dee Dee, Henceforth Free* — so I connected my new bird to the book's protagonist and realized Dee Dee already had completed step one of the formula to quick celebrity status.

As socialites Kim Kardashian and Paris Hilton know, the first step to achieving worldwide fame is to attach your inherited name to an outside event or circumstance and then immediately embrace the ensuing popularity. Both women created sex tapes. Instead of hiding from them, they exploited their experience, name, and notoriety. Now they are both famous just for being infamous, their new businesses surviving artifacts of fame. Boasting nearly eighteen million Twitter followers, Kim offers to Tweet your message to the world for a mere ten thousand dollars. Paris will sell you perfume, boots, and watches. Her sales have topped the billion-dollar mark. So emulating several not-so-accomplished stars, Dee Dee decided to jump start her career with a book deal. She signed a contract to pose for pictures as the main character, Dee Dee, in a children's book. Step one to fame? Latch on to a moving train. Accomplished!

Step two: celebrities require quirky personalities. If they were quiet, reserved, and normal, they would not stand out. Therefore, actor Tom Cruise thought it perfectly normal to perform an interpretative dance on Oprah's couch. Movie star Alicia Silverstone felt comfortable telling her blog followers in a video that she feeds her son, Bear Blu, by chewing up his food herself and then putting it back in his mouth. Yuck! Actress Lindsay Lohan thought it was a reasonable risk to shoplift jewelry, and boxer Mike Tyson thought it was just part of the game when he bit off his opponent's ear. Perhaps Tyson took advice from heavy metal vocalist Ozzy Osbourne. The eccentric singer once visited the offices of a Los Angeles record producer, pulled a live dove out of his pocket, and bit off its head.

Dee Dee stands firmly against bird-on-bird violence, but she reveals her own quirky personality on occasion.

"Nancy, I think Dee Dee might be mentally ill," I worried.

"Why? What's wrong?"

"She just sits there and won't come out."

"She's just brooding," said Nancy. "I think she wants babies."

"Well, I took her out of the nest," I explained. "She sprinted, ran around in circles three times, clucked like crazy, and then pecked the dog on the nose."

Ah! It all became clear. Dee Dee was performing the Tom Cruise interpretive dance. Step two? Check.

The dog is no danger to Dee Dee and her sister Flip. The fourteen-year-old bichon frisé took her obedience lessons to heart. She barks at the pair occasionally, but only because she wants to play. Her playful noise scares the birds, evidence that the cliché *chicken* — as a derogatory term for people who are easily frightened and afraid — is an accurate metaphor. One Saturday afternoon it became obvious Flip and Dee Dee found trouble. They were searching for worms among the blades of backyard grass. I stood with my back turned to them, donned in farming jeans, a shovel over my shoulder. *Clucks* began flying. *Bawks* reverberated against the trees. *Honks* shot into the sky. I turned to see a diving hawk, flying so fast that his image was a blur. The wind of his wings pushed warm against my face. I heard the oh-so-silent bass of his feathers fanning the summer air.

My quick turnaround frightened the predator away, and finally, the hawk became a clear image as he fled east, graceful, and hungry. Meanwhile, Flip and Dee Dee took refuge under the deck, stretching their necks to giraffe proportions, trying to look tall and formidable. Still young and embracing her youthful adventures, Dee Dee managed to check the third step to fame off her list; she suffered through a near-death experience and horrific trauma. Now she can mesmerize the masses on late-night talk shows. Resisting the hawk, Dee Dee stashed away, by default, an NBC up-close-and-personal television script that will precede her eventual debut as a high-jumper in the summer Olympics. She also earned the right to an appearance with late-night host Jimmy Fallon.

"What did you think when you saw those talons reaching for you?" Jimmy will ask.

"I was scared and let out a *'cluck*-you,'" Dee Dee will answer, "but I learned a valuable lesson. Eat like a soldier in Gideon's army. Forage with one eye and scout with the other."

Dee Dee's trauma rivals stories from stars like Gary Busey of *Lethal Weapon* fame. He suffered a motorcycle accident that left him in a coma for a month. And legendary Beatle Paul McCartney survived a near crash in his helicopter, living to tell his story to the *Daily Mail.*

Now Dee Dee has leveraged her near-death experience into a signature head move that delights press photographers. When she sees a shadow, she turns her head parallel to the ground. One eye looks straight up into the sky, the other directly down.

Vanity is step four on the road to fame. Dee Dee plays to her strengths. Some critics have described her as "matronly" and "plump," but when she crosses the road, she waddles her hips with a swagger that Annette Funicello could never achieve. Her golden feathers glisten in the sunlight, a source of pride to her royal Orpington ancestors. Her brown eyes melt the hearts of Brazilian men. Stately tail feathers protect her delicate, velvety down, a covering so soft and beautiful that it serves Dee Dee as a plush pillow even in the rockiest of terrain.

American celebrities know they have to look good to maintain their popularity. They are vulnerable to face lifts and excessive hair coloring. However, a small physical flaw can become endearing, a unique trademark that fortifies their celebrity brand. Actress Jennifer Garner is beautiful, but suffers from brachymetatarsia, which, in non-technical language, translates into an odd, overlapping pinky toe. Celebrity Vince Vaughn is missing the tip of his thumb.

Comedian Stephen Colbert sports a misshapen ear, the result of surgery for an ear tumor when he was ten. In winter months, Dee Dee suffers from a skin condition that puts a chalky white coat on her earlobes. She never spends any time looking in the mirror, so she has never let it bother her. Still, like the star she is, she preens her feathers constantly, putting on sufficient glamor for the camera in her own humble way. Put a check mark next to vanity, step four.

The final rung in the ladder to worldwide fame is to embrace a cause. It must simultaneously do good and push the star's image to the forefront of global media. For actress Jane Fonda, opposition to the war in Vietnam put her on the front pages of all the newspapers. The singer Sting cofounded the Rainforest Foundation and got press. Pierce Brosnan of the James Bond franchise fights the Navy's sonar systems. He worries that the sounds harm whales and dolphins. Environmentalists love him. Dee Dee's cause is organic food. She practices what she preaches, laying eggs — healthy, nutritious, and beautiful ovals with a light-brown shell. If she were to visit a neighbor's house, she would lay an egg. When she is not showboating at a school assembly or off to a photo shoot, she will retreat and lay an egg. Every time she gives an egg away, she sparks a conversation. People talk about her and thank her for her organic diet of spiders, grass, and watermelon. Once, when she delivered a double yolk, the news spread on Facebook and Twitter. Step five to fame? Mission accomplished!

One early evening, a rare break between Rotary appearances and radio interviews, Dee Dee strutted down from her nest, just having delivered another low-cholesterol ovum. She waddled toward me and jumped upon the arm of a patio chair. I pulled out my camera, another chance for photos to illustrate the children's book. Dee Dee flew up higher and wrapped her warm reptilian claws around my camera. Then she stooped her neck and gazed into my eyes as if to peck. Instead, she intimated her own insecurities: "Will I really be the world's most famous chicken?"

"No amount of planning prepares you for life's turns," I said. "The secret, my dear hen, is to be yourself in your own yard. Be kind to your sister. Eat up the mosquitoes. Cluck only after eight in the morning. No one can resist a well-mannered hen. Fame's formula is a self-fulfilling prophecy, and a million Facebook 'likes' are just one good deed away."

About **NCPA**

Northern California Publishers & Authors (NCPA) is an alliance of independent publishers, authors, and publishing professionals centered in the Sacramento area. Its purpose is to foster, encourage, and educate authors, small press publishers, and others interested in becoming authors and publishers.

The association is home to many awarded-winning writers, published authors, aspiring writers, and small publishers committed to becoming the best force to network, pool knowledge, share resources, educate, monitor the industry, and exploit new publishing and marketing media.

NCPA hosts monthly meetings, an online discussion group, professional development events, and an annual awards contest.

Visit the NCPA web page at www.NorCalPA.org.